The Last War Cry Of The Communists

By: Msgr. Gaume

CONTENTS.

— ••• —

FIRST LETTER.

SECOND LETTER.

THIRD LETTER.

FOURTH LETTER.

FIFTH LETTER.

SIXTH LETTER.

SEVENTH LETTER.

EIGHTH LETTER.

FIFTEENTH LETTER.

SIXTEENTH LETTER.

SEVENTEENTH LETTER.

EIGHTEENTH LETTER.

NINETEENTH LETTER.

TWENTIETH LETTER.

Contents.

PREFACE.

WE have read these letters of Monseigneur Gaume with much pleasure, and congratulate the Rev. Father Brennan on the good and even elegant translation which he has made, and now presents to the public. No words of ours are likely to add any thing to the interest with which his work will be read, or to the profit which may be gained from it.

It seems to us that the publication of the letters in our language will be attended with two very important results. It will awaken the reader to the alarming facts of which many of us are ignorant, and which threaten great evils to society. Infidelity has become very bold when it dares to rifle the grave, and exult in driving the consolations of religion from the dying-hour. The attempt to deny God and His providence goes to the extent of thorough atheism, and makes man only a clod of the earth, with no higher hopes than those of the beasts that perish. In our own country, no legislature has as yet sought to prevent the recognition of God at the tomb, or disturb the rites of Christian burial. Yet men who call themselves *intelligent,* are discussing the immortality of the soul, as if it were an open question, or yet to be proved. And we have seen articles in leading journals in favor of burning the bodies of the dead, and thus putting an end to what they call the physical evils of cemeteries.

The second result which should flow from the knowledge of facts so startling, is a truer fidelity to that religion which alone can protect all that is most dear to man. Since the Protestant reformation, we have seen every article of faith denied until there is nothing left of Christianity. Its protection over our lives and its care for the dead, which came from the incarnation and death of the Son of God, are both taken away by that license of private judgment whose true name is unbelief, or the rejection of the supernatural. No creed can stand, no revelation be preached, no light shine beyond the grave, but from " the pillar and ground of the truth," which rests on Jesus Christ, and the verity of His divinity. Those who will not accept atheism, with its sad havoc of all that is noble or moral, must return to the safe shelter of that Church which can never change, but in her dispensation is like her divine Founder, " the same, yesterday, to-day, and forever."

T. S. P.

New-York, March 26, 1874.

INTRODUCTION.

It may be necessary to explain briefly the title of this little work, *The Cemetery in the Nineteenth Century*.

But a few months ago, I concluded my last work, *The Angelus in the Nineteenth Century*, with the following words: " Those who honor me, says the Blessed Virgin, will have life everlasting. With this consoling thought, I now take leave of you, my dear friend, and lay down my pen; for my day is drawing to a close : advesperascit, et inclinata est jam dies."

These were the concluding words of what I intended to be the last will and testament of a long literary life. But my young friend, Frederic, at whose request I wrote *The Angelus, The Holy Water, and The Sign of the Cross in the Nineteenth Century*, refuses to let me rest. On his return, a few days ago, from an extended tour through Belgium

11

and Germany, he wrote to me, saying: " A man may revoke his last will and testament at any moment before death. Thank God, you are not dead: and although ripe in years, are not old. It is not honorable for the soldier to lay down his arms while the battle is raging, and you know better than I, that the contest between right and wrong is now more fierce than ever. As in the desert of old, Jesus Christ and the devil stand face to face. There is war on all sides. I have found that Germany and Belgium are but brigades in that grand army of evil, called the *Revolution*, whose hordes are to be found in every country, both of the old and new world. It is a war of extermination; for, as in the ancient combats of the gladiators, but one victor can remain upon the conquered field. The avowed object is the utter extermination of Christianity, with its institutions, doctrines, maxims, and traditions.

" We must fly to the defense of each point of attack. Permit me then, my dear preceptor, to direct your attention to that exposed point for the capture of which, the enemy has, up to the present time, used strategy; but which he is now assaulting by open and violent warfare. All Catholics are deeply interested in its defense ; for what spot is dearer to them than the home of their dead, the consecrated cemetery ?"

Defend the cemetery! What is Frederic dreaming about ? Where is the sense or reason of such an undertaking ? What connection is there between a cemetery and the great questions of the day? Such were my first thoughts on reading my friend's letter. But after some reflection, and examination of facts, my wonder took flight, and I began to understand the value of the strategic point which I was called upon to defend. Summoning, therefore, to my assistance all Catholics—prelates, priests, and people—I will mount guard at the sacred portals of our Christian Cemetery. My reasons for entering on this duty, as well as the explanation of these letters, will be found in the following proposition : The cemetery is the last point of attack in the sanguinary struggle between Christianity and infidelity in the nineteenth century.

Atheism, after having driven God from the birth of man by forbidding baptism, and expelled Him from social life by shutting Him out from the marriage ceremony, would now tear Him away from man's death-bed and grave, by denying to ministers of religion the right to be present at one or the other. The place of burial, instead of being, as it always was, and still is among nations, whether civilized or barbarous, a solemn and sacred resting-place for the dead, is, in the atheists' estimation, nothing but a rubbish-heap; for man, they say, is but a soulless mass of rubbish. To carry out their views, they have invaded and desecrated Christian cemeteries, taken advantage of the timidity or poverty of families, to force upon them funerals devoid of all religion, and paraded their irreligious demonstrations in the eyes of the public, in city and country.

These odious scandals are but the practical result of the theories held and taught by the infidels of our day : such as Atheism, Materialism, Positivism, Socialism, Communism, and " Solidairism." Cast all these excrescences of Liberalism into the alembic ; mix them well together, and you obtain as a result what sensible people call " *The dog who would bury his neighbor like a dog.*"*

To protest, therefore, with all the energy of my soul, in the name of humanity, in the name of society and religion, against this style of animal-burials, now, like suicide, becom-

---

* Enterre-chien.

ing fashionable, is the general aim of these letters.

In perusing them, the reader will discover that these bold attacks upon our cemeteries and Christian modes of burial are but a part in the general plan of destruction intended by the revolutionary party. Whilst learning the true value of a Christian cemetery, and re-freshing our faith in the great truths which it preaches, we shall see more clearly that our courage in defending it must be commensurate with the opposition of the enemy.

THE CHRISTIAN CEMETERY

NINETEENTH CENTURY.

———•••———

FIRST LETTER.

"WAR ON THE CEMETERY!" THE WORD OF COMMAND TO THE
REVOLUTIONISTS—CONFLICT BETWEEN GOOD AND EVIL.—
HATRED TOWARD THE CHRISTIAN CEMETERY—REASON OF
THIS HATRED—TWO OPPOSING DOCTRINES—TEACHINGS OF
CHRISTIANITY WITH REGARD TO THE HUMAN BODY—WORDS
OF TERTULLIAN—PAGAN TEACHINGS—REBUKE OF NAPO-
LEON I.

MY DEAR FRIEND:

You are right: the cry is, "War on the
cemetery!" During the first days of the Revolution of 1789, the cry throughout France
was, "War on the castles!" and immediately
many of the most wealthy, ancient, and
hospitable dwellings were pillaged and destroyed. This was the first attack of the
Revolution.

"War on the cemeteries!" is now the cry of

17

these same revolutionists. The word of command has passed along the line of that anti-Christian army whose rank and file, more depraved and stronger than the outlaws of 1793, gladly obey their orders. To prove the actual existence of this warfare against the cemetery, to expose its tactics, to show its object, how it is identified with the struggle between good and evil, to indicate what we Catholics should do in order to escape defeat, is the object of this little work.

You see at once, as every one must, who has his eyes open, that we are engaged in a mighty and decisive contest between right and wrong. Since the revival of paganism in Europe, a new spirit has influenced the governments, leading them into apostasy, and thence to excess and ruin.

This spirit, in its hostility to Christianity, never ceases to cry out to it in every language : " Get out of my way, and let me replace you. The world is mine ; for centuries I was its king and its god. Driven by Jesus Christ from my throne and my altars, I now expel Him in return. I reclaim my empire. Leave the hearts and souls of the people; leave politics, philosophy, history, science, literature, and the arts. Leave the family, the school, the social life, and the death-bed of man. Make room for me. Thy reign is over, and mine begins."

The evil spirit is mistaken : his reign has begun, and is now well-nigh established.

For where, in the world purchased by the blood of Christ, do we find the standard of His royal authority ? He reigns, governs, and triumphs. *Christus vincit, regnat, imperat.* Where ? What remains to His spouse, the Church, of her former moral and temporal power? What has become of her influence on society ? Where are her temporalities ? Who owns the souls of her children ? Who presides at the three most solemn and important events in life, namely, birth, marriage, and death ? The spirit of antichrist, so far as he could, has usurped all these in the hope of wiping out every trace of Christianity. " In modern society," say its partisans, "the state is supreme in the birth, marriage, and death of its citizens."*

Hence it must lay claim to the cemetery ; for, if it has the right of regulating man's death, it must also control his burial ; one right is consequent upon the other. Besides, the Christian cemetery disturbs the spirit of evil ; for it is a preacher, the power

---

* Journal de Gand, January, 1873.

of whose eloquence shakes the very foundations of the satanic structure of incredulity,
sensuality, and materialism. His mouth must
be closed at any cost.

As you desire, I will relate the various and
tortuous windings by which this old serpent
is getting into the resting-places of our dead,
in order to profane and destroy them.   To
understand his mode of attack, you must go
back through the whole history of the human
family to the first breaking out of hostilities.
Two opposite influences have been at work
in the world; the divine and satanic.   Without this dogma, which is held in some form by
all people, nothing can be explained.   Having conquered man in Paradise, Satan inaugu-
rated his power and his service upon earth.
By falsifying man's notion of truth, he established paganism, or, as St. Paul terms it, " the
times of ignorance."   (Acts 17 : 30.)

In the fullness of time the Sun of Justice
rose above the horizon, and as it appeared
upon the eternal hills, *illuminans tu mirabiliter
a montibus æternis*, Satan and his agents fled;
the darkness of night gave place to the light
which broke forth and shone on humanity all
over the world.   This was Christianity.

Thus, ever since the fall of man, there have

been two oracles in the world—the oracle of truth and the oracle of falsehood Two fathers, founders of two different citadels— Satan, the father of lies, the founder of the citadel of iniquity and implacable enemy of man, *homicida ab initio;* and the Word made flesh—founder of the citadel of virtue, Creator of all things, Redeemer of fallen men, the Way, the Truth, and the Life; *Via, Veritas, et Vita.*

Our Lord and Belial, Christianity and Paganism, being thus diametrically opposed to each other, you will understand how very differently they must regard the human body during its life as well as its resting-place after death. Christian teaching engenders a profound respect for man's body and requires a sacred place for its burial. Pagan teaching, begetting a hatred for a dead body, demands its immediate removal to any common pit or sewer, or, as the Scripture says, "to be buried with the burial of an ass, rotten and cast forth without the gates." (Jer. 22 : 19.)

Let us hear what these two oracles have to say : " Man's body," says the Christian oracle, is the visible masterpiece of the Creator. The Word made flesh is its type. It was created very differently from all other created beings, no matter how excellent they may be.

They were the effect of an imperative and spontaneous fiat, while the human body was formed and shaped by God, after mature reflection and a council held by the three Divine Persons. Divine Omnipotence, Infinite Wisdom, and Boundless Love, directing their eyes toward the body of the Second Adam, come together and fashion the body of the first Adam, after uttering those words so expressive of the incomprehensible dignity of our bodies : " Faciamus hominem ad imaginem et similitudinem nostram." " Let us make man to our own image and likeness."

Such is the body of man in general. What is the body of the Christian man ? St. Paul tells us that nothing is more deserving of our respect than the body of the Christian. He calls it the vessel in which we carry God, and glorify Him ; the living temple of the Holy Ghost, a member of Jesus Christ, and the inheritor of His glory.

Elevated into a supernatural state by baptism, it becomes the medium of sacramental grace to our souls. When laid in the grave, like the seed sown in the soil, it is to await a glorious day of resurrection. And often, while awaiting its eternal triumph in heaven, it is placed upon our altars and made the object of our respect and veneration.

The respect which the Church manifests toward the bodies of her children is a necessary consequence of the doctrine of Christianity, as is also her exclusive right to their burial, and to the ownership and guardianship of her cemeteries. You know that this triple right was universally recognized for many centuries.

But our modern nations, having turned their backs upon Christianity, and returned to paganism, of course Christian sepulture must be paganized, desecrated, and brutalized; for the greatness of the fall is in proportion to the height from which we descend. The secularization of Christian funerals in the bosom of communities once Catholic, is openly and insolently demanded by paganism, liberalism, materialism, and solidairism; for they are all one and the same vile thing.

Boldly denying the divine origin of man, as well as his future immortality, they utter the most absurd, most contradictory propositions concerning the development and evolution of an improved breed of monkeys, and the migrations of souls. With them, a lifeless body is an object of aversion, to be got rid of as soon as possible, by police regulations, and out of regard to the public health.   From these premises is deduced the whole pagan system and manner of sepulture.

Let me rebuke them in the words of Napoleon I.: " I can pardon many things, but I detest an infidel materialist.   How can you ask me to have any thing in common with a man who, not believing in the soul's existence, proclaims himself a clod of dirt, and wishes to consider me a similar clod ?"

' To-morrow we shall see how these soulless " clods of dirt" succeeded in befouling our cemeteries.

SECOND LETTER.

MY DEAR FRIEND:

Strictly speaking, it was in the last century
that active measures of hostility were directed
against the rite of Christian burial. The "philosophers" of that dismal period, true to their
pagan training, were loud in their demands
to have the peaceful abodes of the dead removed from proximity to the dwellings of the
living. Solicitude for the public health was
the mask behind which they carried on their
warfare. "The cemeteries," they said, "were
hot-beds of contagious diseases; they must
be removed unless we wish the dead to kill
the living," and lying and false arguments,
backed up by lachrymose petitions, were at
once brought to bear upon the civil authorities.

The answer to these objections was simple
and easy. It was only necessary to defy these

25

pretended philanthropists to cite a single example, in all Europe, of any disease arising
from proximity to a place of burial. Usually,
in Catholic countries, the cemetery surrounded the church; God had His field adjoining
His house. Even in the warmer countries,
Rome, for example, the dead have been buried
in churches, and yet no detriment to public
health has ever been discovered to arise from
this custom.

"There is no doubt," says Bergier, "but
that it is right and proper to protect cities and
towns from all danger of contagion. Why,
then, if you are sincere, do you allow so many
taverns, gambling-hells, and other sinks of
moral and physical corruption to exist? any
one of which is a thousand times more fatal
to the well-being of your citizens than the
presence of the harmless dead! However it
may be in cities, we maintain that in the open
country, where the air has room to circulate,
there is absolutely no danger."*

You see, my dear friend, that the removal
of the cemeteries, demanded by the infidels
of the last century, was, as it is to-day, only
a vain pretext. "Permit me," says the Abbé
Proyart, "to declare that in the town where

* Bergier, Diction. Théolog., Art. Cimetière.

I was born, and where the burial-ground is shut in by three houses, one of which was my father's, the inhabitants of these very houses were remarkable for good health and long lives. I remember that, just at the time when these materialists were most afraid of their dead brethren, and loudest in their clamor to send them far away, a judicial inquiry was instituted, at which it was proved that the inhabitants of the houses surrounding one of the worst-regulated cemeteries in Paris, were all in excellent health, and lived as long as their more wealthy neighbors of the healthiest parts of the city."

Under this pretended anxiety for the public health lay concealed a malicious rebuke to the Catholic Church. This careful mother, whom centuries had looked up to as filled with solicitude for the spiritual and temporal welfare of all her children, poor and rich, stood charged with culpable negligence.

Besides, the removal of the cemeteries was an effectual means of speedily smothering every sentiment of devotion for the dead. Bury your friends far away, inclose them with a high wall. lock the gate, and how often will it be within your power to visit the resting-place of your nearest and dearest relative?

Let there be no sensible, sacred sign or symbol to remind us of a departed fellow-being,
and he will soon be forgotten : *Cum sublatus
fuerit ab oculis, cito etiam transit a mente.*
" When he is taken away from the sight, he is
quickly also out of mind," says the author of
the *Imitation of Christ.*

Another motive actuating these Epicureans was, to take away all sad and solemn
thought suggested so forcibly by tombstones,
in order that they might enjoy their illicit
pleasures without fear or remorse. In fine,
separate the church and cemetery, and you
disturb one of the most beautiful and useful harmonies that religion could establish.
Within a small compass you had the three
churches united : the Church triumphant, the
Church militant, and the Church suffering.
What a touching lesson of fraternal charity !
Within the temple you find the Church of
heaven ; that is, the living God amid His angels and saints, really and truly present. At
the altar-steps you see the church on earth in
the crowds of prayerful worshipers ; while
within the shadow of the sacred edifice calmly
sleep the members of the church of purgatory ; our parents, brothers, sisters, and neigh-

bors; silently admonishing us of our duties, or begging our prayers.

To rebuke the Church; to lessen, if not to entirely extinguish, devotion for the dead; to blot out the remembrance of their own last end; to break the golden chains that bind together the children of the Church on both sides of the grave; such was the object which the Voltairians of the last century hoped to accomplish by disturbing and removing the homes of the dead. All the rest was merely an excuse. But the civil authorities of the times preferred falsehood to truth, especially as it was hostile to Christianity.

In order to put its designs into practice, the evil spirit lost no time in incorporating its ideas into the law of the land After its triumph in the French Revolution, it hastened to enforce the following measures, contained in the decree of the 23d of Prairial, year XII, (June 12th, 1804:)

ARTICLE I. "No interment shall take place in any church, temple, synagogue, hospital, chapel, nor any other inclosed building in which citizens are accustomed to meet for divine service; nor within the corporate limits of any city or village."

ARTICLE II. " There will be provided, out-

side of each city and village, at a stated distance from their corporate limits, a plot of
ground, devoted exclusively to the burial of
the dead."

By these two flourishes of the pen the spirit
of paganism abolished the time-honored, wide-
spread, unquestioned, and perfectly harmless
custom established by the Catholic Church,
of keeping near herself her departed children,
that she might pray over their graves as she
had watched at their cradles. This custom
she could not revive without incurring severe
penalties; so stifling her indignation, and her
love for her children, and waiving her own
convenience and theirs, she was compelled to
submit under protest. Should she seek rare
exemptions, she must fall at the feet of the
politicians of the Revolution, who can refuse
or grant her prayer, as they please.

I will place before you, as a memorial of
this despotism toward the dead, the circular
addressed to the Bishops of France by one of
the ministers of Louis Philippe: "To his
Majesty belongs the sole right of granting, in
very rare cases, and under the most extraordinary circumstances, an exemption from the
prohibition contained in the decree of the 23d
of Prairial, year XII. Thus it was that but

recently the remains of certain prelates were interred in their cathedrals, by special permission of the King. However, a recent occurrence has been brought to my notice, which would seem to indicate that, in some localities, these prohibitory laws are not known; and that the inhabitants consider themselves at liberty to bury, as previous to 1790, in their churches. I notify you that if such pretensions are made in your diocese, and be acceded to, it will be considered a violation of the burial laws established with a view to public health. I beg you, Monseigneur, to instruct the ecclesiastical institutions and religious communities of your diocese that, if this be repeated, the civil authority will take steps to remove the remains to the public burial place, and to impose upon the responsible party the penalty prescribed, namely, a fine of not less than sixteen nor more than fifty francs, and imprisonment for not less than six days nor more than two months."

Fearing that the bishops would not prove docile enough, the same minister forwarded a similar circular to the prefects, adding: "The town officers not having power to authorize burials anywhere but in the public cemeteries or private burial-plots, at the legally prescribed

distance from the towns, will be held responsible if they permit them to take place in the
churches. I request you to instruct them to
this effect, and to remind them of their re
sponsibility."

What was the result, my dear friend, of
this first campaign of modern impiety against
Christian sepulture?

You have it in a few words. The Church, as
a perfect society, had enjoyed during the middle ages all the rights peculiar to a perfect
corporation. Of all her rights, the one least
questioned was her right to legislate in the
matter of burying her own children; that is,
the right of owning and governing her cemeteries. The demon of heathenism raises its
head, and "philosophers" come forth to call in
question every ecclesiastical right and privilege. The Revolution confiscates them all,
enacts oppressive measures, and forces them
upon the Church. She submits to this new
outrage, hoping for a return of law and order.
Vain is the hope.

Infidel constitutions are framed and everywhere adopted. Freemasonry, now become
master of the situation in the large cities,
seeks to overthrow the supernatural order,
and, consequently, the destruction of conse-

crated burying-grounds. It has lately demanded, in Paris, the still further removal of
the cemetery to a distance of thirty miles from
the capital; and to hasten the measure, it
hints at the early necessity of burning the
dead Parisians.

However, in this universal war of paganism against Christianity, the removal of the
cemeteries was, as you have already discovered, only the first step. The second was to
get possession of them. The circular given
above supposes this seizure already accomplished, and is nothing more nor less than
the application of the first, seventh, ninth,
tenth, and eleventh articles of the Prairial decree. Although in former times all cemeteries, with rare exceptions, belonged, in Catholic counties, to ecclesiastical corporations,
the law declares to-day that all places of
burial belong to the civil power, that is, to the
politicians. It does not allow an ecclesiastical corporation even to acquire title to a piece
of land for burial purposes. Even in cases
where the civil power held title to a cemetery,
its government was always intrusted to the
Church; as were the questions of baptism,
marriage, and death. This was all changed
by the politicians of the Revolution.

Moreover, the right of ownership implies the right to use and regulate : third and fourth step in the revolutionary invasion. To the mayor, then, or some other political office-holder, of no religion, or who may be an atheist, Jew, Protestant, materialist, or a member of the Society of the "Solidaires," belongs the sacred right of keeping guard over the homes of our departed brethren in Christ. He is to appoint the hour of their funerals, and designate the spot where their bones may be laid. Our pastors, the real and true fathers of their flocks, must be silent and obey. All that is left to them is the negative right to absent themselves from the obsequies of a public sinner who has died impenitent. But what scandalous and violent vituperation has been hurled against the clergy, who, availing themselves of this right, refused to sanction the wickedness of sinners' lives by being present at their funerals! The revolutionary press of France and Belgium have wasted more ink and paper in their diatribes against the clergy for refusing to assist at the funerals of public sinners than would suffice to transcribe the whole *Summa* of St. Thomas.

These seizures of Catholic cemeteries by the civil authorities are founded on the first and chief principle of the Revolution, namely, complete and perfect equality of all religions, true or false.

Previous to the triumph of pagan materialism in 1790, Catholics, Jews, and Protestants had their own respective places of burial ; but the revolutionary party, having inscribed upon their banners and law-codes the principle of liberty, and equality for all religions, must logically establish one common cemetery for the believing Catholic, for the denying Protestant, and for the Jew who laughs at both.

Retaining, however, some very slight sense of shame, the decree of Prairial, while permitting but one cemetery for all classes, graciously consented to have separate sections set apart for the use of the different religions ; such sections to be separated by a ditch or hedge, and each to enjoy a distinct entrance.

Hence, within one inclosure, you had several distinct cemeteries; death keeping up the religious separation that had existed during life. When an unbeliever died impenitent, his remains were interred in an unconsecrated spot. This was tolerable.

These distinctions were distasteful to the " solidaires ;" for on the one side, the dread of a dishonorable burial deterred many from join-

ing their sect, or led them to forsake it just
before death.   On the other hand, it was in
direct opposition to the latest theory of
" solidairism," that is, general and promiscuous mingling of good, bad, and indifferent
in death, as these " solidaires" desire to have
also during life.

What did the Communistic town-officers of
Belgium do?   Availing themselves of their
power, they opened a campaign against the
custom of excluding impenitent reprobates
from any part of the cemetery, and went to
work and forcibly interred " solidaires" in consecrated ground.   This they did in Brussels
and in Gand.   In this latter city, the town-
officer, on his own private authority, placed
the ancient consecrated cemetery under inter-
dict, and established a new one of his own.
In vain did the bishop protest.   The town-
officer replied that, although burial was an
affair appertaining to the civil power, yet he
would graciously permit the ministers of all
denominations to perform their respective
rites at the graves; and called upon the bishop
to come and bless each grave at a time.   The
bishop's reply was, " You wish to compel the
Catholic clergy either to consecrate each grave
separately, or to consign the bodies of their

spiritual children to unhallowed soil. Catholics can not shut their eyes to this open and unwarranted violation of their rights and insult to their faith. Your system deprives the cemetery of its religious character, and treats as a common field a place for which Catholics have ever entertained feelings of reverence and awe. It strips the burial rite of all its spiritual meaning, deprives the faithful believer of a comfort highly prized by him—that of laying his bones in the midst of the household of the faith ; where, while awaiting the day of resurrection, he may enjoy the suffrages of his church.

" You are willing to permit us to bless the graves separately. This is not freedom enough for our ritual, and we will not accept it. In pagan lands, and in regions where it is impossible to have cemeteries, or to exercise public religious functions, the graves of deceased Christians are sometimes thus blessed. Even in Paris and other large towns, where the interments in the cemeteries, of infidels, Jews, heretics, criminals, and outlaws exceed in great numbers those of the Catholics, this custom is followed of blessing the single graves. Except in these cases, the practice is unknown. What is merely an exception to law and order and custom, you wish to transform into a general and continued practice, sanctioned and required by the civil law. If once admitted, there soon will not be a single Catholic cemetery in the whole Church."

You perceive, then, that it is the design of the " solidaires" to hasten the destruction of Catholicity, by attacking it in one of its most vital parts, that of Christian burial. Their attempts have been partially successful, for very many towns are now without any place for Catholic burials. It is time for us to bestir ourselves, and to raise our most decided and energetic protests against this wholesale trampling under foot of our ancient rights and privileges.

Besides being denied the privilege of burying her children where she thinks proper, the Church is not permitted to indicate the mode nor yet the hour of their funerals, as you will see by the following circular, bearing date the fourth day of the month Fructidor, year XIII, and addressed to the various prefects: " I transmit to you the decree of the fourth of Fructidor, commanding the civil officers not to allow the clergy, without special permission, which permission they must be able and ready to show, to go to the house of a deceased person, or to be present at any portion of the obsequies, except shut up within the walls of the church."

These orders were rigorously enforced, and to disobey them rendered the party liable to fine and imprisonment. These were only the preliminary attacks of the revolutionary party. Their further invasions of our cemeteries will be seen in subsequent letters.

THIRD LETTER.

MY DEAR FRIEND:

What action was taken by the revolutionary party when they had secured possession of our cemeteries? The action which they ever take, when brought in conflict with religion: to desecrate, ruin, and efface. In the peaceful times, when Christian influence prevailed among the people and their rulers, you could hardly have found in town or country, a palace or a cottage whose roof was not surmounted by a cross, or its front embellished by a statue, picture, or pious emblem. For graver reasons, the cross, the comforting sign of our future resurrection, was invariably planted as well on the lowly graves of the poor as on the mausoleums of the rich.

40

Under the reign of pagan impiety, the cross was turned into a weathercock, and the statues of the saints gave place to lewd images of pagan divinities. The graves within the churchyards of the large cities were so completely dismantled that it would be impossible to say whether Christian or Jew, man or beast lay beneath the heaving turf.

And even this sad privilege, now for the first time heard of, of placing or of omitting the sign of salvation on our graves, was not long enjoyed. Soon we saw the enemy, in a paroxysm of anti-Catholic hatred, pulling down and shattering the crosses, breaking the tombs, tearing open the coffins, plundering them of valuables, and scattering the ashes of the dead to the four winds.

Who does not shudder at the remembrance of the sacrilegious profanations during the revolution of 1793? Pagan antiquity never witnessed, never would have tolerated, never conceived such desecration. The sacred and solemn precincts of the tomb were invaded, and the leaden coffins dug up to be turned into bullets. In the church of St. Denis, the tombs of the French kings, objects of respect and veneration for centuries, were reduced by the pick and hammer in the hands of vandals, to a heap of unsightly rubbish. In their pagan hatred of the dead, they allowed their boys to play at foot-ball with the skulls of kings.

The revolutionary spirit is the same to-day as it was then. With the same implacable and undying hatred of Christianity, it persecutes it to the bitterest extremes in its cemeteries as in its churches. Thus in the month of April, of the year 1873, a deputation from the municipal government of Seville, coming before the cemetery, forcibly wrested the key from the hand of the reverend chaplain, entered the sacred grounds, and took down every Catholic image and emblem. They then tore off every cross, even where it involved gross mutilation of the handsome and costly monuments.

Nor was pagan vandalism content with destroying Christian ornaments. It polluted the graves, by placing over them its own silly emblems, and engraving upon the marble ridiculous infidel inscriptions and devices. On one side you meet Mercury, the god of thieves, flourishing his rod ; in another place, Death, with his menacing scythe ; and again, old Father Time and the inevitable hourglass. Here are broken columns, veiled urns, shafts, pillars, cones, and figures containing devices emblematic of geographical or mathematical research. Hideous owls stare at you from the tracery on the headstone, a formidable cannon threatens you from a pedestal, swallows make vain efforts to wing their way to the skies on marble wings, while Cupid, with inverted torch, hovers and presides over all. These are but a few of the absurdities thrust into the sacred home of the Christian dead.

Here are a few of the countless inscriptions in which nonsense and naturalism contend for ridiculous supremacy: " Here lie buried all my hopes, all my joys, all my sweetest comforts." " Adieu, obedient daughter, faithful mother, kind sister, adieu: often will I come to sit on this cold stone and dream about you." " To the memory of A, wife of B, real-estate holder." " To Isaurus, deceased in the twenty-second year of his age. My God, to die at twenty-two! too soon! What have I done to die so young! I had not yet learned to live! No time to fulfill my destiny! Who will care for my poor mother?" Whilst grieved at the utter absence of all Christian sentiment, we are disgusted at the want of common sense. Read these words, graven beneath a sculptured butterfly : " Take thy flight heavenward, and there dwell for all eternity with thy family which has preceded thee." Decipher these if you can, and then admire their depth and beauty of sentiment.

What will you .hink of this inscription, placed over the grand entrance to a well-known cemetery : " Death is an Everlasting Sleep "? Could Greek or Roman heathenism be more scandalously, plainly, and openly expressed, or a grosser insult be offered to our sacred and solemn rite of Christian burial ?

Shocking as these profanations are, they sink into insignificance when compared with the appalling aims of the revolutionary party, and the terrible means they employ to attain them in France, Belgium, and elsewhere. Catholics are not given to suspect dangerous attacks from their fellow-men ; indeed, they are too submissive, have too much respect for law and order, and the powers that be ; are too willing when struck on one cheek, to turn the other. They should be warned of the danger, roused to a sense of their outraged rights, and learn what they have to expect from freemasonry, " solidairism," paganism, and liberalism, as boldly taught in our godless schools.

The design of the enemy is to convert our consecrated cemetery into a vile pit of corruption. Later on, we shall see why.

Meanwhile, study the stratagems employed to accomplish their ends. Witness what is taking place to-day in one of the most important cities of Belgium. The mayor of Gand, himself a freemason, has just suppressed, on his own responsibility, and contrary to law and reason, a cemetery belonging jointly to six Catholic parishes of the city, by forbidding within them any further interments. "After the first of January, 1873," says the order, "all interments from the six parishes whose cemeteries have been expropriated, must be made in the common field provided by the city government." Observe that our worthy mayor does not disturb the graveyard of the Jews or Protestants, whilst for that of the Catholics he substitutes a common receptacle unhallowed by any blessing, save such as a politician and freemason can impart.

By virtue of his office and title of " inspector of common receptacles for the dead," this man officiated at the opening of his common sewer ; marching and countermarching during a whole day, uttering his ejaculatory orisons.

All who have the honor of his acquaintance
know from what liturgy these prayers are
taken. After having announced that the
sink was prepared, and that henceforth citizens
could bury free of expense, whomsoever and
whatsoever they would, he concluded his consecration by a violent diatribe against the
clergy.

This opening discourse was a fitting pre-
lude to the words of blasphemy that will come
from the foul-mouthed orators of the free-
thinking school when presiding at the civil
funerals of their fellow " clods of dirt," deceased. In this vile place, with its political
or masonic blessing, baptized Catholics, whose
bodies have been the dwelling-place of the
Holy Lamb, whose members are still moist
with the consecrated oils of extreme unction,
are to be thrown, in indiscriminate confusion,
with outlaws, heretics, and infidels.

In order to give the sanction of law to
this promiscuous mixture, the mayor issued
a circular informing the keepers of the common field, that they were privileged to allow
any and all inscriptions to be placed upon the
tombs; from the De profundis, down to the
blasphemous motto, " True peace of soul
consists in denying the existence of a God."

The next thing is to supply matter to be decomposed in his caldron; so his tax-paid mourners are eager for a funeral, or, as they would say, an opportunity of performing chemical experiments on the rotting " clods of dirt." On the last day of the year, just as the prohibitory act had closed the gates of the Catholic cemetery, a good and respectable citizen died. His had been the edifying death of a Christian, and his last request was to be buried in consecrated ground. But the next day the politicians held the keys of the Catholic cemetery, and the friends of the deceased learned, with grief and indignation, that the gates were closed against them. Notwithstanding the cost and inconvenience, they resolved to carry the remains of their departed brother to the graveyard of a distant parish ; saying that if it took their last cent, they would not have him buried like a dog. The money was soon raised to defray the expense of the unexpected journey, the hour was fixed, the *cortége* went to the church. Meanwhile, " The Common Inspector of Cemeteries" was preparing to officiate as high-priest over the grave. When, after the religious services were ended, the funeral procession was seen to turn its back upon the Potter's Field, and go in another direction, there was evinced a subdued but heartfelt satisfaction on the part of the neighbors. Restrained by the sacredness of the occasion from shouting applause, they uncovered their heads, waved their hats in the air, and as a still further protest against political graveyards, many journeyed the whole distance to the Catholic burial-ground.

This is all very melancholy, my dear friend. Just to gratify the sentiments of hatred for religion, entertained by a handful of free-thinkers, all our liberties are sacrificed, our convenience disregarded, and our family invaded in its most holy relations, and in its most solemn moments of affliction.

You ask, how long will this state of things continue? As long as the pagan demon of liberalism shall hold sway, and that will be as long as we keep up a system of pagan education in our godless schools.

In the next, more about these invasions of right.

FOURTH LETTER.

MY DEAR FRIEND:

It is true that steps were immediately taken
to legalize these unauthorized proceedings
of the mayor of Gand, and a society was
formed in Brussels, having for its object to
secure the adoption, by law, of this principle
of secularizing sepulture, and of making its
practice general. This secularization would,
of course, lead to a general mixing up and
ignoring of all religions, or rather to a denial
of any religion at all; just what the party of
the revolution are seeking. The people of
Gand taking no pains to conceal their horror
for animal-burying, every thing is done to
stifle and stamp out this Christian feeling.
We hear constantly of the perpetration of

49

acts of the most heartless cruelty to force
these people to consign their dead to the
Potter's Field.   It is labor lost.   For the
people will resist, telling the bailiff, as they
do, " If you are so fond of your common sink,
go bury yourself in it."

While the wealthy can easily escape the
rayless gloom of heathen sepulture, by repair-
ing to the distant graveyards of the rural parishes, the poor feel the whole weight of this
Communistic tyranny.   This will always be
the case.   In every war waged against religion,
the poor are ever the first to suffer.   We
know of a thousand incidents each more
touching than the other, and all proving the
high appreciation that the masses of the
people have of the dignity and sacredness of
Christian burial.

A laborer, who had died in the hospital, had
begged that his body might be claimed after
death by his neighbors and given Christian
burial. Who is to pay ? The poor neighbors
raised the required amount by subscription
among themselves. Boundless examples of the
same kind might be adduced to show the un-
willingness of the people to be buried like cattle, and associations are formed to procure, by
private subscription, as well as by appeals to

the public, the means necessary to enable the poor to carry their dead to the distant churches for Christian burial.

The Catholics of Belgium are doing still more, for they are unceasing and fearless in their resolute and decided protests against the execrable tyranny of the " solidaires." I will quote a few, for it is well to know how to speak and act if the party of revolution should ever gain the ascendency over us.

The Freemasons, becoming convinced that their Catholic neighbors would not submit to be thrown into a pit like dead cattle, demanded that each grave should be separately blessed, saying that this would settle at once and for-ever all difficulties in the matter of sepulture ; or, if any future misunderstanding arose, it would come from the clergy, and they would be held responsible.

Alas, the poor priests! If their rights are trampled, if they are robbed and put to death, they only get their deserts, for are they not the cause of all our trouble ? So say now, as pagans always said, the enemies of truth, peace, and order. I am here reminded of an anecdote, very *à propos* to these unfound-ed charges. A sturdy citizen of Paris, fol-lowed by his dog, was passing in front of a market where game was sold, and near the door of which stood a cage containing live rabbits awaiting their approaching fate. Just then a rabbit protruded his nose between the bars of his cage, and the dog making a sudden snap, bit off a portion of the nose and ran away. The store-keeper, startled by the cries of the wounded animal, pursues the man, seizes him, and demands payment for his rabbit. On the indignant refusal of the citizen, who had been totally unconscious of the occurrence, the injured merchant threatens an appeal to the police-court. " Say, mister," said an urchin, " let him arrest you. I saw how it happened, and if you give me a few cents, I will go witness." " What will you say ?" said the citizen. " I'll swear the rabbit began it !"

The Bishop of Gand, following in the footsteps of his illustrious predecessor, has been pleased to reply to the insolent suggestion of the " solidaires," to have each grave blessed as it is about to be occupied. His words are those of an intelligent man who knows his place, and is calmly conscious of his rights and duties, and who knows how a bishop ought to speak and act. In his communication to the mayor, he writes : " It would now seem that your resolution is taken not to seek the blessing of the Church for your new burial-ground. Hence it will not be established in conformity with the statute of the twenty-third of Prairial, nor be such as the Catholics enjoy throughout Belgium, France, and other countries, except a few localities where, owing to extraordinary circumstances, a blessing could not be given. Can we not come to some agreement in the matter? You propose a separate blessing at each grave. This, you must be aware, I can not grant. I am not at liberty to act contrary to what the discipline of the Church prescribes, nor to dispense with a general law. To do so, would be to transcend my powers as bishop in a case where the Pope alone has power of dispensing.

"The matter can be settled between ourselves. Request and permit me to bless one portion of the new cemetery for the exclusive use of Catholics. . . . By seeking this blessing, you will remove all difficulty, and afford unspeakable satisfaction to the inhabitants of Gand generally, with the exception of a few whom nothing would satisfy."

To this generous, condescending, and modest communication the haughty mayor returned an absolute refusal. What else could we expect? In all countries, the self-styled apostles of liberty, once they obtain power, become ruthless despots.

The following protest, from an eminent magistrate, met with the same fate as that of the bishop. " Apart from the matter of hygiene, and the respect due to the memory of the dead," writes a judge of the Court of Appeals in Brussels, " the sepulture of men, the conditions, manner, and form of such sepulture are essential parts of worship. As religion affects man chiefly in his relations with the life beyond the grave, he would be untrue to his nature, if he kept silent in a question occupying so important a place in his concerns as the separation of the soul from the body. There can be no worship, nor liberty of worship in denominations, if they are deprived of full freedom in every thing regarding doctrine, hierarchy, and discipline, nor unless they are themselves their own judges."

To the appeal of reason, succeeds the cry of an outraged conscience. You will be pleased to hear, as I certainly was delighted, these words coming from the eloquent lips of one of those noble Christians who are an honor to Belgium, and who, with God's will, will be her salvation.

" According to your offensive system of burial laws, the Catholic funeral service is virtually abolished. This is a flagrant violation of liberty, and we therefore protest against it. Obedient to your laws when they are not contrary to our honor, nor to our consciences as Catholics, we raise our voices against an act of tyrannical injustice whereby we are deprived of a consecrated cemetery, and a funeral service in conformity with our ancient liturgy, and have violently forced upon us a common field where we must consent to be buried like cattle which have died of the plague. Nay, more, you go further; for you grant full license to your friends to come to these very graves, and there insult our faith and blaspheme Christ. This is what you call enlightened government ! thus to reduce to an intolerable state of slavery a population eminently religious.

" If there are to be found among us some baboons, over-fond of consigning their highly developed and fully evolved organizations to a political grave-digger for interment, we find no fault with their fanciful free-thinking. If our worthy mayor wishes to be buried in the Zoölogical Garden, and near the monkeys' cage, or perhaps would prefer to be stuffed and placed in a glass case in the museum, he need not apprehend any opposition on the part of the statute of Prairial to interfere with such grave eccentricity.

" Do not force us to accept a system so much at variance with the laws of the Catholic Church, so opposed to faith, to our most time-honored traditions, to our inmost affections. What you are now doing is not simply an injustice; it is wicked and offensive; it is infamous, and must cry to heaven for vengeance. If you had to deal with a less obedient people than are the Catholics, you would soon see public indignation giving a fitting rebuke to your provoking measures by deplorable but natural violence.

" Do not deceive yourselves, however. Although we are not in favor of violence, nor admirers of the 'uprising of the people,' yet, we are fully determined to defend our rights by every peaceful and legitimate means. It must not be said, that a hundred thousand Catholics tamely submitted to a Jacobin's iniquitous ukase. They must make a resolute and united resistance. It is time that we should cease to be patient, when patience becomes folly. We must drive the vampire of 'solidairism' from our midst, and take up arms in defense of our fathers' graves as well as of our own.

" Enjoy then, 'solidaires,' your dismal funerals; but let us have the comfort of Christian burial." *

This, my dear friend, is the way to talk to these people. Would that these words could infuse courage into the hearts of all Catholics. If their acts correspond to these words, the victory is theirs.

---

* M. J. De Hemptine, dans le Bien Public, 25 Jan. 1873.

FIFTH LETTER.

MY DEAR FREDERIC:

Travelers, in their ascent of Mount Vesuvius, frequently meet with crevices in the
rocks, giving forth small volumes of heated
smoke. The Italian guides call them "*fumarole,*" and tell you that there is fire beneath the
smoking embers. We find these "*fumarole*"
throughout Belgium and France. Wherever
we turn our steps, we tread on these smouldering embers, and see these small clouds of
smoke, betokening the existence of subterranean fire ready to burst forth at any moment, with the fury of a volcano. The whole
army of the revolution has received the word
of command, " Attack the cemeteries !" and it
is panting for action.

Let our bishops, priests, and laity be ready to receive the enemy's assault. Hitherto we have been defending, in the open field, our outer breastworks; namely, our religious, charitable, and educational institutions. The enemy has taken them and is now battering at our inner works, the cemeteries; and then will come the assault upon our citadel, the churches themselves. If we falter, all will be lost; for Communism in the graveyard means communism in the churches; that is to say, one church for all kinds of worship, or rather abolition of all worship.

The revolutionary party knows this result, and is working to accomplish it. I have already told you that, hitherto, persons dying out of the communion of the Church were buried in Catholic cemeteries, but in a section reserved for such cases. This is fair enough; inasmuch as persons whose choice it was to separate themselves from Catholics while in life, could hardly be over-anxious to be with them in death.

Modern infidels do not take this view of the matter. They call this distinction an inroad on human liberty, an outrage to their tender consciences, a wounding of their feelings; and they know it to be a rebuke to their odious theories. They must reform this abuse at any price; and they are now at work striving to abolish what they call "the reprobates' corner."

Now, what do they want? I repeat that they want to exclude from the cemetery every Christian thought, all belief in positive religion, all faith in immortality, all hope of resurrection. They want to humiliate and insult their Catholic brethren, by placing heathenish and masonic emblems side by side with our crosses. They want to shock the feelings of good men by uttering the impious blasphemies contained in the burial service of the "solidaires."

Now, this is what we do not want. We will not have impious men to stand over our fathers' graves now, nor over our own in future; and, whilst our bodies are awaiting the resurrection, to spew out, in their vile funeral discourses, horrid blasphemy about "*the darkness of the Gospel*," and to treat as "*vulgar errors*" the most sacred dogmas of our faith.

This, my dear, is the latest stage of the campaign carried on by the pagans in Belgium, that "land of the free," against Catholic sepulture. Although a little in the rear, the revolutionary armies of Switzerland, Italy, and

France, are marching, under similar orders, to the same point of attack. In Italy, the cemeteries have already fallen into the hands of the state authorities, and been placed in the keeping of a municipal officer, who may be an unbeliever, a "solidaire," or a highly developed " clod of dirt." All the customary sacrileges of course accompanied this seizure.

For example: no less than four civil interments have taken place in one town within a few days ; and, in every instance, against the wishes of the deceased, who had died Catholics, and of the relatives who protested vigorously, but in vain, against this violation of liberty of conscience.

But this is not all. To wipe out all trace of the Catholic cemetery, and to silence forever its truthful and warning voice, Italian liberals now cry out for the burning of the dead. This is the logical consequence of their education. True to their training, they believe that pagan antiquity is the highest and most perfect type of civilization. Ancient Rome, the Rome of the Cæsars, the metropolis of the great republic, burnt her dead. We must do the same, if we wish to be considered fully civilized.

Thus it is, as our Holy Father, Pius IX.,

truly observed, the infidel party is leading paganism back to Italy over every highway and by-way. You are aware, my dear friend, that an official request to have the dead burned, was recently made in the Italian Parliament, assembled at Rome; and made by a liberal physician, Maggiorani, himself a Roman. Yet there are many who refuse to admit the disastrous results of the study of the ancient heathen classics.

How common an occurrence it is now, since the Italian invasion, to meet these civil funerals in the streets of Rome! You remember, of course, the case of the wife of the radical journalist, Bottero. According to the notices posted up on the street-corners, inviting the " solidaires" to the funeral, " she died as she had lived, a true patriot." Her remains were carted to the burial-ground, without any emblem of religion, and infidel orations were pronounced over the body, in presence of her husband and children. In this manner, the most ancient and hallowed cemeteries, containing the sacred ashes of the very first martyrs of Christianity, are again and again defiled. These scandalous excesses, unparalleled in Christian history, are perpetrated by the liberals in order to pollute the holy city, to de-

fy in his imprisonment, the head and repre-
sentative of Catholicity, to deny the truth of
Christianity in its very stronghold, and to
prove that henceforth Communism is to be
king in Rome.

Ungodly and profane, or, as they call them,
civil burials, are common enough in Switzerland, that hot-bed of infidelity; and yet the
liberals are not satisfied. Among the modes
of persecution, practiced for the last few
months in that country, is an effort to compel Catholics, at all hazards, cost what it
may, to discontinue religious observances at
their funerals, and to bury their dead in the
common burial-ground.

The National Assembly of Berne, in its ses-
sion of the 12th of September, 1873, declared:
"The state, with every thing appertaining
thereto, is under the jurisdiction of the civil
authorities. Ecclesiastical jurisdiction is here-
by abolished. The right of providing and
regulating cemeteries belongs solely to the
civil authorities. Therefore the cantons will
provide suitable places of burial, which will be
accessible, at all times, to all persons deceased
within the corporate limits."

Among the hardy mountaineers of Jura,
who for so many centuries enjoyed, in undis-

turbed tranquillity, the practice of their faith,
religion has been reduced to a private worship.
No public ceremonies can be performed, the
church bells are silent, and the chant of the
choir has ceased. The priest is not permitted
to carry the blessed sacrament openly, even to
the dying. When a parishioner dies, his pastor may proceed, in the garb of a private citizen, to the house, and there read in subdued
voice the solemn prayers of the ritual; but he
must not accompany the funeral procession in
his official capacity. The liberal government
graciously permits him to celebrate a low
mass, but requires the closing prayers to be
said privately in the sacristy. Then the remains of the Christian maiden, or of a pa-
rent, whom the priest has baptized, instruct-
ed, loved, and cherished in life; whose eyelids he has closed in death, are carried out
without priest, prayer, or cross, or any of the
ancient ceremonies to which these faithful
Catholics have been accustomed. The body
is lowered into the grave in silence; for the
church must not intrude herself before the
public gaze, to pronounce those last prayers,
so consoling to the living, and so useful to the
dead.

But the worst is to come. For modern

paganism in that country has been bold enough to demand, and strong enough to obtain, an order for the expulsion of the clergy from their parochial houses. Even now, we see them seeking shelter in the private homes of their flocks; and very soon we shall meet them in their hurried departure from their native land, exiled, hunted down, and hounded into caves and forests, as in 1793. Once the clergy are out of the way, the Jura will witness grim and dismal funerals according to the cheerless ritual of unbelief; the sacred homes of her dead will be polluted, and liberalism will shout for joy.

I will say nothing, my dear Frederic, about your own Germany, much less of Prussia. Berlin, the headquarters of Communism, internationalism, "solidairism," and paganism, will soon witness the godless burials of those things which they wickedly term "Chemical compounds in a state of dissolution."

Why was France, too, drawn into the anti-Christian movement? Why? Because, forgetting her glorious mission, as a leader among nations, she prostituted, to the service of impiety, her noble and powerful faculties. Like many another nation, she presented the poisoned cup of paganism to the lips of her children, and they got drunk, and thus became hostile or at least indifferent to Christianity. She has repudiated the glories of her past history, driven Christ from her doors, and admitted the devil through the window. This is the secret of her humiliation.

The following letters will show you the workings of these deplorable pagan theories in France.

SIXTH LETTER.

MY DEAR FRIEND:

We have been admiring the achievements of the anti-Christian army over the dead in Belgium, Spain, Italy, and Switzerland: let us now hear from France.

But twenty years ago, an unchristian burial was a thing unknown amongst us. Now it is an every-day affair, not only in Paris, but throughout the provinces. Amongst the most notorious and scandalous was that of "Ste.-Beuve," who has been so lauded for his bare-faced denial of the divinity of our Lord; and another, that of a young girl lately deceased in St. Philip's parish. In the latter case, the death was thus shamefully announced in the funeral invitation: "You are invited to the funeral of Miss N——, who has just died in the fourteenth year of her age, her virginity

67

undefiled by religion." There was lately another of these dismal affairs in the Montmartre district; that of a teacher and female apostle of materialism. She was followed to the grave by three hundred " no-God " people, dressed in white, with bouquets in their hands, and her own husband had the bold, bad taste to deliver an address over the grave, praising his beloved wife for having chosen to die without priest and without faith. Only a short time ago, no less than six godless interments took place in one day in the cemetery of Père Lachaise; each one embellished by a blasphemous harangue. The following choice language was heard over the coffin of one woman : " Dear fellow-citizen, we thank thee, in the name of our association, for the good example thou hast given, by living and dying a freethinker, that is, a pronounced and bitter enemy of the clergy and despotism." Thus one soulless clod addresses another.

Paris fashions must be followed. So you may now witness, in most of our large cities, similar bold and open exhibitions of impiety; public protests against all religious belief, at once shocking to the spectator, and degrading to the liberals themselves. Proud of its rapid advancement, encouraged by a forbearance of which I will not venture to speak, liberalism but lately had the insolence to claim from the authorities public recognition at the funerals of its adherents. Thank God, it received a well-merited rebuke.

You have not yet forgotten what occurred last June at Versailles. Posterity will be loth to believe that among the legislators, intrusted with the sacred duty of lifting France from the degradation to which she had been brought by anti-Christian, anti-social denials of truth, any would be found perverse or blind enough to demand the payment of official honors at the funeral of a colleague who had died professing doctrines subversive of religion and society. You know of whom and of what I speak.

A legislative member, named Brousses, after having been all his life a libertine, died a " solidaire." Those members of the legislature who were of his way of thinking thought it a favorable occasion to make a practical parade of their theories. Having succeeded in obtaining the consent of the members to attend the funeral, they hoped to force France herself, in the persons of her legislators and soldiers, to sanction their wretched and desolate theories. They reckoned without their host.

Although they had sent notices and invitations without number, there were not more than fifty persons at the place of meeting, exclusive of thirty-five or forty "*representatives*" of the people who came with much parade, bearing their parliamentary insignia.

According to custom, the vice-president of the Assembly, accompanied by two secretaries, had repaired to the house of the deceased, while two companies of cavalry, detailed to do military honors, were stationed before the door. But as soon as the members saw the procession issue from the door, the corpse carried by members of the "solidaire," and not the least sign or mark of religion—nothing to remind one of the departure of a soul—they turned their backs upon this indecent exhibition of atheism, and withdrew. The military officers immediately gave orders to their soldiers to follow the example ; thus leaving these misguided infidels to carry out their disedifying demonstration by themselves.

On reaching the cemetery, one of their number saw fit to insult the people's faith, by giving his own and the deceased brother's views on the animal whom they claim as their father ; assuring his hearers that they were nothing more than a good breed of domesticated monkeys. To utter such expressions in the very teeth of state officers, brought thither by official etiquette, and of soldiers, whose duty required their presence, seemed to these self-styled animals a very master-stroke of cleverness. It would be a semi-official contradiction or negation of the Catholic faith and piety, gloriously manifested in our present miraculous pilgrimages.

You may well imagine, my dear Frederic, that our free-thinkers were exasperated at their failure. They could not conceal their bitterness, and on the very next day, they arraigned the legislative body on a charge of infringement on the rights of conscience, and of contempt for the law. But they had not to wait long for an answer. It was proved as clear as the noon-day sun, that no law had been transgressed, either in spirit or letter, and that liberty of conscience had nothing to do with the question. To add to their comfort, a full *exposé* was made of the odious measures resorted to by these people, in France and Belgium, to obtain subjects for these beastly burials.

Two statutes of the first Empire were cited by the infidels to prove that there had been a violation of the laws. These enactments or-

dain that public and official funeral honors
shall be conferred upon any member of the
Tribunal and Legislature, deceased in the discharge of his duties; and that the body shall
be accompanied to the cemetery by the military, who shall discharge a farewell salute over
the grave.

The defendants, whilst admitting the statutes, required their adversaries to show, if they
could, that these honors were to be paid to
any persons, except those who had died, and
were to be buried according to the rites of
some religion.   Now infidelity, instead of being a religion, is the denial of every religion.
Although the enactment was made on the
twenty-fourth day of Messidor, in the twelfth
year of the Republic, it never entered the mind
of any one, not even of Napoleon himself,
to decree honors to those who chose to be
buried like dogs.   It would be unjust, nay,
monstrously so, to expose the feelings of the
Catholic legislators, and the dignity of the
military to the mercy of these infidels, who,
whenever one of their number should chose to
die as a brute, could exact the presence of their
respectable Catholic colleagues at their irreligious demonstrations.   What!   If one of these
free-thinkers, who maintains that he is an

ape, should take a notion to have his brethren, the monkeys of the Zoölogical Gardens,
attend his funeral, must our brave soldiers escort them as guard of honor?

Disgracefully beaten on the ground of ille-
gality, the "solidaires" appealed to their rights
of conscience. Their adversaries replied:
" You have no right to assume that you have
a conscience. You believe that all men, including yourselves, are nothing but living
dirt, soulless creatures, with no higher destiny
than to gratify your appetites. You can not
have a conscience, for there is no conscience
in a heap of dirt.

" But why seek to obtain honor and respect
for a mere clod of earth? Why expect men
to bow before animals? If you were consistent, you would summon the members of your
fraternity around your death-bed, inform them
that you are only a decomposing piece of
matter, returning to its original elements; that
all is over with you forever; that what people
call remembrance, is only a relic of ancient and
worn-out ideas about exploded immortality.
That there is no more a devotion for the dead
than there is for God. Tell them to go to
their business on the day of your death as on
any other day, only take care to give orders

that when the rubbish-cart passes, your body shall be carried away with the other garbage of the house."

Such, my dear Frederic, ought to be the language of a true and consistent materialist; and if he do not act according to his own views of death, he has no right to demand respect for his opinions, nor to say a word about conscience. He would not be a true materialist, but only a sectarian, ready to insult the conscience and faith of his fellow-man. He deserves no respect, and can lay claim to no freedom; to freedom of conscience less than to any other. Not believing practically in his own carcass theory, he must deserve only contempt and extinction.

However, the more clearly we show that mere matter has no conscience, and can not have any, the more persistently do these soul-less people clamor about freedom of conscience. "Freedom of conscience!" That is their watch-word and rallying-cry. How easy to rout them on their own battle-ground!

They do not know the meaning of the words, liberty of conscience. Indeed, in the strict sense, it is a contradiction in terms, and therefore false. There is nothing in man less free than this conscience, or less independent of his will or of his caprice. What is conscience? Conscience is an internal practical judgment, prompted by God, whereby we decide whether a thing is right or wrong, and which we must necessarily obey. We can not act contrary to its dictates without sinning. We have no freedom of conscience in act, word, or thought; it compels us to follow the right. External acts are qualified by the intention. They are licit or illicit, meritorious or criminal, according to the thought whence they proceed. This interior faculty, this inward light, man could no more create than he could make the light of day which enlightens our eyes. He sees it—can not shut it out from his vision. For the eye of conscience is without eyelids. It can not close its eyes, and withdraw itself from the illuminating ray of moral truth.

To be sure, man can abuse the organs and faculties given to him by God. He may put out his eyes, and thus leave himself in darkness. But would this be liberty? Perhaps it would be liberty of self-mutilation, or the liberty of the suicide. Every effort made to deprave conscience, to put out its eyes, is a mutilation or moral suicide. We are not at liberty to play with or abuse our conscience, but to preserve it in a sound, healthy condition as it came from God—a condition which we call a *right* conscience—conscientia *recta*—and which we are never free to disobey.

SEVENTH LETTER.

MY DEAR FRIEND:

God has been pleased, in accordance with the laws of divine wisdom governing the world, to turn to good account this disgraceful exhibition at Versailles. It became the occasion of giving utterance, within the very halls of the French legislature, to truly sublime Christian sentiments. I would call your attention to the noble declaration of General Du Barail, Secretary of War.

A "solidaire" had charged him with violation of law in ordering the withdrawal of the military from the funeral. "You pretend to think," he replied, with all the vigor of a soldier, "that this was a transgression of the laws of my country, but I assert that it was a vindication of those laws. Soldiers obey the

army regulations. Now, the 374th regulation
of the military code directs that soldiers, detailed for the purpose of rendering funeral
honors, shall proceed to the late dwelling of
the deceased, to escort the body first to the
church, and thence directly to the grave. By
the *church* all men understand a temple of
religion. In no case could we permit our
soldiers to be identified with irreligious demonstrations, or implicated in open acts of impiety. If you tear from the soldier's bosom
the hopes of a better life, how can you ask
him to sacrifice his life on earth in defense of
yours ?"

At these words, the "solidaires" winced in
silence, but the loud and hearty applause of
the majority proved, to the general's satisfaction, that he had nobly and successfully vindi-
cated the honor of the army and the faith of
France.

But the account was not yet settled. These
loud-mouthed champions of liberty of conscience were put to the blush before the eyes
of the civilized world, by seeing their odious
transactions dragged into the light of day.
This duty fell to the lot of the Minister of the
Interior. Furnished with many well-authen-
ticated facts, he proved that these people had

set up a new trade, and actually trafficked in the poverty of their fellow-men, in order to get material for their anti-religious exhibitions.

He assures us that the civil interments, which took place in Lyons, were not from choice on the part of the deceased or their relatives, but were the work of organized societies, who, having money and political influence, had it in their power to repeat, several times a day, these outrageous proceedings. This organization is called the "Society of Free-Thinkers." They repudiate all religion, and pledge themselves to protect their members, or all whom they can in any way influence, against the interference of the clergy in all affairs of body and soul. Members are required to attend the funerals of their brethren, or suffer a fine. During its triumphant reign in Lyons, in the days of the Commune, this fraternity had decreed a fine of fifty francs upon any priest presuming to attend a funeral."

There can be no funeral without a corpse, and notwithstanding their pretended numbers and great influence, these fellows could not induce many to accept them as their undertakers. They therefore established a traffic in the bodies of the poor. A host of facts can be adduced to prove that a cruel and unprincipled advantage was taken of the inability of the poor to defray the cost of burial, and that they yielded under strong pressure from the " solidaires." At the four civil funerals which took place in Lyons in one day, all the bodies had been secured from the city alms-house.

Now it is a widow, unable to protect her husband's remains; now an orphan. who can not defend his father's corpse ; and then some divorced husband, who returns after his wife's death to allow and secure an interment according to the civil custom. Even the bodies of infants are made the occasion of infidel demonstrations.

Here is a very revolting case. A boy of twelve, who had made his first communion, died a few hours later, after a short sickness; whereupon his unnatural father permitted the society to bury his child, and to defray the expense. More than four thousand persons, headed by the mayor, his assistants, and several other functionaries, took part in this demonstration. Other instances might be cited where young people, with the reluctant consent of their impoverished parents, were thus buried like animals, only a few hours after having partaken of the Body and Blood of

Christ. The warden of the Lyons alms-house asserts on oath that out of twenty-four who had been buried from that institution by this infidel society, twelve had expressed a desire to receive the rites of their church before death, and even protested against being buried as animals by any anti-religious society.

The police commissioner of the same city of Lyons has also stated, that, during the last twenty months, he was called upon at least a dozen times to interfere in cases where the families of deceased parties were being constrained by these Free-Thinkers to have their dead buried without any religious rite or ceremony.

The mode of proceeding was this. As soon as these meddlesome infidels heard of a death in a poor family, they would repair to the proper departments of the city, get the permits, order the grave and coffin, pay for every thing, and then proceed to the apartments of these poor people, and sometimes by bribery, and sometimes by threats, get an unwilling consent to inter the corpse after their own fashion. In some cases, the relatives were actually driven by these fellows from their own homes, and had to appeal to the police for protection, in their efforts to save the bodies of their nearest and dearest from what they considered a horrible desecration.

Let "solidaires" now prate about freedom of conscience. Is it freedom of conscience to abuse the poverty of a dying fellow-creature, to take advantage of family secrets, of an infant's helplessness, an orphan's destitution, a widow's distress, and of the terror inspired by a bold and powerful combination of unprincipled men?

They ought to be ashamed to pronounce the word liberty; or rather, they ought to be afraid—for they have no shame—lest the word should stick in their throats and choke them.

Our memories are not so poor as to make us forget the exploits of the Communists, who made it a crime punishable with death to wear a cassock. Nor have we forgotten the famous Cadet, and the premium he offered to atheism during the Commune by issuing the following notice : " Any citizen who shall have died without asking for a minister of religion, will receive civil burial at the expense of the corporation." To put some limit to the dreadfully demoralizing effect of this tempta-tion thus presented to the poor, the new pre-fect, as you know, issued the following :

" Article I. Every certificate of death pre-sented to the city authorities of Lyons, must be accompanied with a second certificate, stating whether the body is to be interred with or without the ministrations of some clergy-man belonging to one or other of the re-ligions recognized by the state. This second certificate, bearing the applicant's signature, will be placed on record, as a guide in the ap-plication of the regulations contained in the following article.

" Article II. Except in very rare cases, where the mayor may decide, all burials unattended by any religious rite must take place as fol-lows: From the first of April to the thirtieth of September at six o'clock in the morning; and from the first of October to the thirty-first of March, at seven o'clock A.M. The rest of the day is reserved for religious fune-rals.

" Article III. Funeral processions must fol-low the least frequented streets, unless they have a special permit from our office to pass over a specified route."

Our free-thinkers had hardly got through gnashing their teeth at these orders, when another quickly followed, limiting the atten-dance at funerals to three hundred persons,

and forbidding all meetings within the places
of burial.

But these restrictions imposed by the authorities had not much effect on the liberals.
Although compelled to obey the regulations
of the street-cleaning department, requiring
all garbage to be removed from the streets before a certain hour in the morning, yet they
continued to make their unwholesome demonstrations.   As a reply to the prefect's orders,
they buried a member of the free-thinkers'
fraternity, aged eighteen months, another aged
two years and six months, and a third, who
was an old bachelor, aged thirty-six.   This
last was to be a test case, in which they hoped
to bid defiance to the law limiting the atten-
dance.

But they reckoned without their host.   For
when the *cortége* was formed and ready to
start, the officers of the law counted three
hundred, and then cut off the tail of the
procession.   Do not imagine that they ac-
knowledged themselves conquered.   By no
means.   The restrictions of the authorities
only irritated them, and during the month of
July sixty *beastly* funerals were seen in the
streets of Lyons.   "Solidaire" funerals, like
suicide, seem to become epidemic.   Nothing

perhaps, we may say *en passant,* shows more clearly the utility of our correspondence. The horror which must thrill you, my dear Frederic, as you read these lamentable details, will never equal the shame, grief, and fear that I have experienced in writing them.

Throughout France, Belgium, and many other countries, are to be found vast organizations of men and women, who claim the honor of being clods of dirt, and of proclaiming all their neighbors to be similar soulless clods; with the public press advocating their views, professors expounding their doctrines, legislators sustaining them, and encouraging them to vomit out their abject theories in the face of honest men. And this is where we stand after eighteen centuries of Christianity. Can optimists find any thing like this in past ages?

EIGHTH LETTER.

Genealogy of the "Solidaires"—Man an Educated Being—Remarks of a Missionary Bishop—Two Systems of Education, the Divine and the Satanic, Christian and Pagan—The "Solidaires" taught by the Pagans—Proofs—It is a Mistake to attribute the Rise of Rationalism to Protestantism—Proof—Something about Luther.

My Dear Friend:

Whence have these people come who are now endeavoring to make sepulture a public teacher of materialism by transforming our cemeteries into pits of corruption? Who ever begat these beings, holding and diffusing opinions from which the most audacious blushingly recoil and regret that they are human? As a necessary step toward remedying the evil, we must first solve this question. The solution is in the two following propositions:

First proposition: Education makes a man what he is. Be he Catholic, Protestant, Jew, Mohammedan, or heathen, he is what his education made him: nothing more nor less.

A few weeks ago, I had a visit from a Canadian bishop who had been twelve years a missionary among the Indians. During his visit, he remarked: "If my Flat Heads and Esquimaux had been born and brought up in France, they would be Catholics. And if they are not, it is because they did not receive a Catholic education. If they are savages, they owe it to their savage training. Say and do as you will, a man is what his education makes him." Nothing is more certain.

Second proposition : Ever since the fall of man, two systems of education—one good, the other bad—have, side by side, accompanied humanity, forming individuals and nations. Which system has produced the evil of "solidairism"? The Christian system? Certainly not, for a doctrine teaching that man is a soulless heap of earth, the descendant of an ape, a mere animal, can not be found in the whole Christian system. On the contrary, you know as well as I, that this and similar absurd theories have ever been condemned by Christian teaching.

"Atheism must then be the result of evil or pagan education," you say. Yes, necessarily and logically it must. For we find their doctrines more or less plainly taught in the

pagan authors.   The Sophists of Greece and
Rome were apostles of doubt, and destroyers
of all ancient beliefs among men.   Up to their
time, says an old writer, the traditions of
revelation existed in some form.

Now, these pagan authors have been for
centuries, and are to-day, the admired models
of youth, and of that class of youth who,
by their superior position, must necessarily
lead the opinions and fashion the minds of
men.   Every body knows that "solidaire"
theories had not their origin among the lowly
and the unlettered.   It came, and it is coming
to-day, from those who have drunk deeply of
the poisoned cup of pagan classical literature
—the graduates of educational institutions.
Previous to the study of these writers, none
of the deplorable evils that we now find everywhere, could be discovered in Europe.   And
if there are infidels to-day among the uneducated classes, they owe their paternity to
the educated, who, coming forth from their
schools, communicate what they have received, and can transmit nothing else.   Libra-
ries, the public press, the theatre, and literature, are their exclusive work, the development
of their classic ideas; each and all being so
many indefatigable agents of the criminal

apostolate. The people read them and are poisoned; and this explains the mystery.

It is our duty, then, to combat a pernicious system, favored, alas! even by Catholic educators. Most people blame Protestantism; imputing to Luther the rise of that rationalism and "solidairism" now ravaging Christian nations. Nothing could be more false. Nothing could be more useless than their very serious attacks directed exclusively against Protestantism.

No one denies that Luther is responsible for much of our modern unbelief. But it is one thing to be the author of an evil and another to be its propagator. We can not assert it often enough, that Luther, the father of Protestantism, did not beget rationalism. He found it existing and applied it to the spiritual order of things by setting his reason above the authority of the Church.

The truth is: firstly, that Luther was just what Leibnitz styled him, a "logical man." When he appeared upon the scene, atheism had been reduced to a system, and freethought having been carried into Europe on the poisonous breath of Greek philosophy, was a full-grown goddess. Fugitives from Constantinople introduced her to the youth of Europe, and soon she counted innumerable admiring followers in all countries, but especially in Italy. Volumes of history might be cited in evidence of this fact; but I will confine myself to the testimony of two or three undoubted witnesses.

Thomasius, an ancient Protestant writer, in giving the pedigree of the rationalists or atheists, uses the following striking expressions: " History proves a strange fact; namely, that, from the time of the overthrow of paganism by Christianity, no atheists were found in Europe, till we meet them in the fifteenth century. On its return to Europe, ancient paganism produces evil results; for we see atheism springing into existence, and then the establishment of a vast school of infidelity in Italy, the very focus of Catholicity. Its founders, professors, and disciples being men imbued with a love for beautiful antiquity, revived ancient errors, banished long before by the power of the Gospel."

Spizelius, another Protestant, who wrote before Thomasius, testifies to the same facts. " Who can deny," says he, " but that the revival of pagan literature in Italy, in the fifteenth century, brought out, cultivated, and developed the ancient theories of Lucretius,

Epicurus, Horace, and others? It was then that a great number of teachers administered draughts of poison to the young, under the name of ancient classical literature."

Bayle, too, attributes the rise of rationalism to the same cause. "Atheism," he says, "was unknown in France until during the reign of Francis I.; while in Italy it broke out during the revival of the classics." He repeats, "I find no atheists in France prior to the time of Francis I., nor in Italy till after the final capture of Constantinople, when Argyropulus, Theodorus of Gaza, George of Trebizonde, with other learned men of Greece, took up their abode with the Duke of Florence. It is quite certain that the learned literary writers, who flourished in Italy at the revival of the belles lettres, subsequent to the taking of Constantinople, had little or no religion."*

It is not to be denied that Luther, like his precursors, the rationalists of Italy, owed his apostasy to his insane fondness for the pagan classics. Hear the testimony of his biographer and beloved disciple, Melancthon: "Luther's soul, in its thirst for knowledge, drank

---

* Diction. art. Takiddin.

from the best and most abundant sources. He read most of the ancient authors, not as a child to learn a language, but to acquire a knowledge and standard of human life."* Indeed, such was his infatuation in this regard, that these profane authors became his inseparable companions; for even when embracing the monastic state, he secretly and clandestinely carried with him into his convent copies of Plautus and Virgil.† His peculiar education had taught him to look upon such authors as very treasures. And he knew no other; for he tells us himself that at the age of twenty he had not read a single line in the Holy Scriptures. And was he any worse than most of our young college students, brought up like himself by Christian teachers, but fed upon pagan literature till their empty heads become intoxicated with the charms of heathenism?

For him, as for many others, paganism effected his ruin. Christian literature, Christian theology, and Christian philosophy, being devoid of the beauties of classical antiquity, were in his estimation simply barbarous.

---

* Vita Lutheri. Melancthon, tom. ii.
† Melancthon, ibid. p. 6.

"Moreover," says Brucker, "he directed all his energy, not only to the disparagement of scholastic philosophy, but to its utter banishment from the schools. There is no doubt but this hostility arose from the same cause as that of the literary people of Italy, who, blinded by their love of pagan classical learning, became unfitted to wear the yoke of scholastic philosophy. Thus Luther, having spent the years of his youth in closely following these ancient authors, affected to be shocked at the rudeness of modern literature."*

Although this ought to be testimony enough, I will summon as a still better witness, Luther himself, who, in a private and confidential letter, thus speaks his mind: "After full deliberation, I have come to the conclusion that it is simply impossible to reform the Church, without first completely abolishing canon law, the decretals, scholastic theology, logic, and philosophy, as we now have them, and building all over again on new foundations." It is, as you see, ever the same story. Pagan antiquity had become the model for every thing good and beautiful.

---

* Hist. Phil. lib. iii.

But the Church, not knowing these schools, and even having refused to recognize their claims, was looked upon as sunken in ignorant barbarism.   A church steeped in barbarism deserves no respect—can not be the true church.   It becomes our duty, therefore, to destroy it if we can.   " How can you expect me," says Luther to Reuchlin, " to believe an assertion coming from the rude tongue or pen of a vulgar fellow who is unable to decline *musa?*"   Such was the reasoning of every pupil of the pagan schools, in matters of religion, politics, literature, architecture, etc.; and in order to remodel the Christian world in a pagan mould, they kindled a revolution the flame of which carried wide-spread desolation.

This question will be further considered in the following letter.

NINTH LETTER.

MY DEAR FRIEND:

We have now come to the critical moment in Luther's life. The fire of paganism which has been long burning in his breast will now burst forth, and we shall see this pupil of the heathen masters open his batteries against the Church, and shake it to its very foundations, in order, forsooth, to rebuild it after his pet model of ancient perfection. It was much in the same way, too, that the revolutionists of 1793 made their attacks upon society, wishing to build upon its ruins a system fashioned after the same model of pagan antiquity.

Hear the biographers of our renegade monk of Wittenberg. "Luther," they write, "having been thoroughly drilled in the ancient pagan systems, became convinced that scholastic philosophy and theology were the source of every error and evil in the Church. He determined, therefore, to leave nothing undone to overturn these systems. Fully apprised of the vastness of his undertaking, as well as of the risk he ran, he hesitates for a moment. But looking up to the great and glorious scholars in Italy, who had already opened a gap in the enemy's defenses, he receives new courage and confidence, and at once opens the attack."

Amid minds already predisposed for the change by those apostles and admirers of ancient paganism, the men of letters, reform in Germany spread like a prairie fire. Brucker tells us that it owed much of its success to Catholic "*littérateurs;*" among the rest to Erasmus, Vives, and Nizolius. All that was wanting was a bold hand to apply the torch. This bold and reckless hand was Luther's.

I do not think, my dear Frederic, that you can find a clearer and truer account of the origin of Protestantism. You have here the cause and the occasion. The cause was the love of ancient pagan civilization; the occasion was the example of men of letters in Italy and Germany.

It is a well-established fact of history that these literary men, while claiming to be Catholics, had, long before Luther's time, openly professed and taught such monstrous tenets derived from pagan writers, that Luther himself never dared to countenance them; for example, pantheism and materialism. The Council of Lateran, held in 1512, five years before Luther published his theses, was obliged to condemn these systems, taken from the ancient Greeks, and to declare the principles of the new philosophy and the revived literature to be poisonous and unsound, " radices philosophiæ et poësos esse infectas." Erasmus, the chief patriarch of the revival of ancient literature, confirms the testimony of Melancthon and other historians, by his brief but expressive remark, " I laid the egg, and Luther hatched it." The Protestants of the seventeenth century, speaking through the mouth of minister Jurieu, corroborate the testimony of Erasmus; for they tell us confidently, " Were it not for the revival of pagan literature, we would not be in existence." In fine, the revolutionists, rationalists, and materialists of our day boast of their descent from the " Renaissance." " We are children of the revolution," say they, "and we are proud of it; but we are still more the children of the ' Renaissance.' "

It is a fact, my dear Frederic, that the rationalists of every sect are unanimous in their praise of this period of revival, which they call " the emancipation of thought." As Brucker has it, " The study of the ancient classics severed the chain which held reason subject to faith, and bound philosophy to authority." It is natural to suppose that these people know where they came from, and they unanimously hail Florence in Italy as the birthplace of their so-called " glorious revolution.

How deeply to be deplored is the blindness of all those respectable and good men who, instead of taking the rationalists' declaration regarding their primary cause, and setting to work to tear out the poisoned tree by the roots, only hack away at its branches! The enemy laughs at such tactics. Notwithstanding your eloquent and learned defenses, the torrent of rationalism carries them away, and is now overflowing both Catholic and Protestant lands. If you would prevent destruction, you must ascend to the source of the stream and dry up its springs. Its fountains, as you know are the ancient classical authors. Unless the study of these men is discontinued in our colleges, labor as you may to stop it, you will have an unfailing crop of materialists and "solidaires," calling themselves animals, living like animals, dying like animals, and insisting upon being buried like animals.

Meanwhile, these infidels are rapidly reducing their theories to practice. Unable to act in their individual capacity, they have formed societies the better to apply their atheistic doctrines to the affairs of practical life. Hence you have Freemasons, free-thinkers, materialists, positivists, "solidaires," and, to crown all, the logical and consistent animal.

These gloomy associations are so many regiments in the grand army of evil, which, if not checked in its advances by the hand of God, will invade and destroy the most sacred institutions of society.

Here again, my dear friend, if you will take the trouble to examine, you will find that the founder, organizer, and director of each and every one of these associations, is not a man from the uneducated classes, but in all cases a man of some learning. The remedy, then, is not to be found in a prefect's proclamation, or in the censure of a legislative body, but in the total suppression of pagan education, and the substitution of a thoroughly and truly Christian training of the youthful mind. Until this change takes place, we are only throwing chaff before the wind. While the revolutionists will laugh at our efforts, sensible men will repeat the truthful remarks of a Protestant of our own time: " It will fill posterity with astonishment to learn from history that an age calling itself Christian, condemned its youth, during seven or eight years of the most impressionable period of their lives, to the almost exclusive study of the pagans."*

We know, my dear Frederic, whence the " solidaires" have come. But where are they going ? What is their object ? In a word, what is the cause of their hatred and opposition to Christian sepulture ? The reply is on the tip of my pen.

Christian burial in a Christian sepulchre annoys them. Why does it annoy them ? Because it is an eloquent and fearless preacher of doctrines opposed to theirs. Wherever the cemetery-cross stands, surrounded by Christian graves, there you have a popular, eloquent, and impartial expounder of truths, raising its voice night and day, in town, village, and country, against the pernicious views

---

* De Gasparin, Intérêts génér. du Protest.

of those who insist upon throwing human garbage into the sewers of a "solidaire."

These disgraceful sectarians, having sunk lower than the heathen of old, lower than the savage of our time, ay, and lower than the brute, claim that man is only a mass of rubbish ; that the soul is a myth, and resurrection a fiction. The effect of such theories would be to free man from all responsibility ; to make no difference between virtue and vice, and to set up the law of the strongest, as the only law in force among the herd of wolves called the human race. Nothing has ever been known more radically destructive of religion, and, of course, of society, than these dreadful theories. Now, the Christian cemetery preaches four truths diametrically opposed to them—namely, the dignity and sanctity of the human body ; the grand law of universal and eternal brotherhood ; the immortality of the soul ; the resurrection of the flesh.

While St. Bernard, St. Chrysostom, Bossuet, and the other grand and mighty orators of the Church can only announce the sublime truths of religion, one at a time, the cemetery proclaims them all in one voice, in a language that all can read, and in tones that penetrate into every part of Christendom. Now you perceive how well founded are the opposition and hatred of impious men.

The cemetery proclaims the dignity and sanctity of the human body. The patriarch Moses, while in charge of the flocks belonging to his father-in-law, Jethro, had penetrated one day into a remote part of the desert, near Mount Horeb, when suddenly he perceived, at some distance from him, a bush all enveloped in flames, and yet not consumed. Wishing to examine more closely this strange phenomenon, he was about to advance toward it, when he heard a voice issuing from the flames, saying, "Come not nigh hither. Put off the shoes from thy feet: for the place whereon thou standest is holy ground." *Locus enim, in quo stas, terra sancta est.* (Exodus 3 : 5.)

The same voice speaks to us from the cemetery, Approach with reverence, for I am holy ground. The Church, by her blessing, prayers, and sprinkling of holy-water, has withdrawn me from the common earth, and released me from the baneful power of the devil, that arch-corrupter of both our physical and moral nature. She has restored me to my native liberty and purity, in order to make me a receptacle, a consecrated reliquary designed to receive and preserve something holy. Not for my own sake have I been purified, blessed, and sanctified; but out of regard for the human bodies that will repose within my bosom.

If we wish, my dear Frederic, to have some idea of the sanctity of our bodies, we may get it from the magnificence of the ceremonies and prayers used by the Church, in her ardent desire to make our graves in some way correspond to that dignity and sanctity.

The explanation of this page of Catholic Liturgy, so little known to men, will be the subject of our next letter.

TENTH LETTER.

MY DEAR FRIEND:

I invite you now to accompany me to the consecration of a cemetery, and while on our way, I will tell you what few persons are aware of—namely, that the consecration of a cemetery is a function reserved exclusively to bishops. This fact alone will give you some idea of the sacredness of the place to which we are going. But lo! see! What a mysterious spectacle! In each of the four corners of the field stands a cross about five feet in height, whilst in the centre we see another much higher. In front of each of these five crosses is planted a stand of less height, and having on its top three sharp points to hold three candles. The crosses and stands were erected but

104

yesterday; for only one night is permitted to intervene between their erection and the august ceremony we are now about to witness. Two vessels, a large one filled with water, and a smaller one containing salt, are set at the foot of the central cross.

I know what thoughts are running now through your mind, my dear Frederic, as well as through the mind of many another spectator. What is all this preparation? What do these things mean? I will tell you. These lifeless wooden stands, resembling the dryness of fleshless bones, represent man in his grave. They were set up yesterday, for yesterday is a figure of fleeting time; and in every corner of the cemetery, to remind us that the empire of death is spread all over the earth.

The three candles not yet lighted represent the imperishable germ of life placed in our bodies, by the three persons of the Blessed Trinity. Soon, at the direction of the bishop, these candles will be lighted, and I will give the mysterious signification of their light.

The cross in the centre of the field is higher than the others, and represents our Lord Jesus Christ, who, having vanquished death, has been made for us the resurrection and the life. He is the first-born among the dead, casting His

protecting and saving shadow over His sleeping children.

This mysterious cross set up in the middle
of the ground proclaims that the Divine Word,
by whom all was made, and all was saved, is
the centre of all things, the King of heaven and
earth, with an empire stronger than that of
death, and extending over the past and the
future, the living and the dead.

From their places in the four extremities of
the field, the four lesser crosses proclaim that
the life-giving blood of Calvary has flowed to
the four quarters of the globe, to bring life
on the day of resurrection to all men, no
matter in what age or clime they may have
died. This is the reason why the wooden
stands, figures of the dead, are placed before
the crosses representing the resurrection and
life.

The candles are lively representations of
the general resurrection. When a fire is extinguished, we say it is lifeless, but alive
when rekindled. If, then, these extinguished
candles reminded you, as they did me, of a
dead man, when we shall see them burning,
we shall see in spirit the man restored to life.
This is the mystery of which I promised to
give you the consoling explanation.

The water and salt at the foot of the cross are to be blessed by the bishop, in order to become holy-water—that powerful element of sanctification.

Now that you know the meaning of the several objects before you, I ask you, if our holy mother, the Church, the great teacher of men, could find more suitable and comprehensive language wherein to proclaim to us such magnificent truths? If it is true that man, whether rich or poor, young or old, is not a pure spirit, and consequently needs, as the Council of Trent says, the assistance of sensible things to raise him up to the comprehension of spiritual things, let the great philosophers who despise our august ceremonies find a more effective means of making us understand truths that are beyond the reach of our senses. As for myself, filled with gratitude and wonder, I will ever repeat St. Teresa's saying, " I would lose my head for the smallest ceremony of the Church."

More beautiful and more eloquent still, if possible, are the prayers used at the consecration of the cemetery. Let us recall a few of them.

Here comes the bishop, preceded by the clergy. He is vested with cope and mitre, and bears his crosier in his left hand. As he advances, all the candles are lighted, as in anticipation of the resurrection, the certainty of which he is to proclaim from this very stronghold of death. After a short address to the people on the sacredness of the Christian cemetery, he begs of God, in a touching prayer, that the bodies of all those here buried, may, on the great day of judgment, arise glorious from the tomb, be reunited to their souls, and admitted to the never-ending joy of heaven.

Having finished this prayer, the bishop, clergy, and people kneel down and recite together the litany of the Saints, begging their coöperation in obtaining the object petitioned for. Toward the last verse, the bishop arises, and making the sign of the cross three times, says, " That Thou wouldst vouchsafe to purify and bless this cemetery, we beseech Thee to hear us : that Thou wouldst vouchsafe to purify, bless, and sanctify this cemetery, we beseech Thee to hear us : that Thou wouldst vouchsafe to purify, bless, sanctify, and consecrate this cemetery, we beseech Thee to hear us."

To prayer and the sign of the cross, the bishop adds a third sanctifying agent, and after having blessed the salt and water, he walks around the four sides of the ground, sprinkling it with holy-water. Returning to the central cross, he prays that when the angel's trumpet shall sound, all the bodies here interred, may arise to enjoy eternal happiness. He then incenses the principal cross, the figure of Jesus Christ, and taking the three lighted tapers from the wooden stands, sets them on the top of the cross. He repeats this last ceremony at each of the four lesser crosses. Thus is proclaimed and professed the belief in a general resurrection to life of all men, effected by virtue and power of the cross of Calvary. Could any thing be more expressive?

Two prayers follow, with a preface of singular beauty, both in style and meaning. In language that might have come from heaven, the Church, by the mouth of her bishop, recounting all the mysteries of time and eternity, reminds her Divine Spouse of all His claims upon her gratitude and confidence; namely, His infinite power, and His equally infinite wisdom, goodness and mercy. She then beseeches Him to bless this cemetery as He blessed of old the tomb of Abraham, the father of the faithful; and as He gave the Promised Land to the Israelites forever, He would deign now to secure to the bodies resting in this spot undisturbed repose, exemption from all desecration, *ab omni spurcitiæ inquinamento*, deliverance from all attacks of the devil, *ab omni incursione malorum spirituum;* and that finally, as He had in the person of Lazarus, who was four days buried, foreshadowed the resurrection of the whole human family, He would vouchsafe to call to a glorious resurrection all those bodies here present which had been purchased by the blood of Calvary.

How sublime an idea of the dignity of Christian burial, as well as of the worth of our bodies, is conveyed to our minds by these admirable prayers and solemn ceremonies! Besides, however, challenging your admiration, reverence, and confidence, they have no doubt excited your wonder; for they evidently suppose that we may be disturbed in our graves by evil spirits. And so it is, my dear Frederic, they not only suppose it, but assert it, and we are bound to believe it. We have not a more authentic monument of the belief of the Church than her rituals and the Roman Pontifical. I may add that this belief in evil spirits disturbing the dead is a portion of the deposit of universal tradition, intrusted to the infallible keeping of our Holy Mother the Church.

In the first place, you must know that the pagans themselves had preserved a more or less confused knowledge of this truth. Not to enter into long detail, I will merely recall to your memory the fear they always manifested of the wicked manes, (*impii manes,*) and the practices they employed to drive them from their tombs. A Greek pagan, in order to defend his dwelling against the attacks of evil spirits, had written over his door: " Hercules, the god of protection, lives here." At a later date, the inhabitants of Antioch, in order to avert the dangers of earthquakes, often the work of the devil, had inscribed upon the walls of their houses, " Christ is here, be still." And to-day, in the very midst of the onslaught of satanic infidelity, we find in the homes of many families, pictures of the Sacred Heart of Jesus, with the words, " Cease, the heart of Jesus is with me." There is nothing new under the sun of the Church. If it is true, then, that evil spirits can trouble the living and haunt their dwellings, why would not God, in His mysterious counsels, allow them the same power over the dead? As we have seen, it is to neutralize this power, that the Church blesses the dwellings of the dead. And she is right; for from century to century, authentic facts prove that God permits the devils, those appalling ministers of His justice, to inflict chastisements on the bodies of sinners.

Among many examples supplied by history, I will cite only the following. In one place, a flame of fire was seen to force its way into the grave of an impenitent victim of lust, and burn up his polluted remains. An instance is vouched for of a wretched, abandoned female, whose body was torn from the bed of death. In Milan, the body of an impenitent sinner who had been buried in a holy spot, was carried off by two spirits of horrible aspect, and thrown beyond the walls of the consecrated ground. Again we read of dragons torturing the remains of unjust kings. Is it necessary to add that evil spirits have the power to clothe themselves in the bodies of the dead, or at least in their forms? How else are we to account for the apparitions, noises, revelations, etc., so well known to day in spiritualistic circles?

The Church knows what she is doing, when using so much solemnity in the blessing of a cemetery. Well aware of the powerful hatred of the devil, she knows that prayer, blessings, and holy-water, which have been safeguards to man during life, are also efficacious after death. Her faith is the faith of ages.

Hence the common practice of burying with a corpse, articles that have been blessed, such as scapulars, crosses, medals, and rosaries. Hence, too, those last solemn words which fall from the lips of the priest at the edge of the grave, *Requiescat in pace;* " May he rest in peace!" This prayer of the Church applies not only to the soul, but also to the body of the deceased ; indeed, to the whole man. It evidently supposes a disturb-ance of man even in the tomb. By whom? By the devil, of course. Hence, also, that short but mysterious inscription found on thousands of the niches in the Catacombs, where repose the bodies of the early Christians, those heroic servants of God, namely, *In pace,* " In peace." Yes, in peace of soul, in peace with the Church ; in peace of body too, placed as it is in earth consecrated and defended by prayer against all infernal agencies; in peace inviolable until the glorious resurrection. Hence, too, in fine, another still more explicit inscription, *Christus hic est,* " Christ is here."

Great is the advantage then for body as well as for soul to be buried in consecrated soil.

Pardon, if you please, this long letter.

ELEVENTH LETTER.

MY DEAR FRIEND :·

What profit should we derive from the
imposing ceremony just witnessed? We
should be moved to compassion, if not to indignation, for those unhappy people of our
times who seek every opportunity and use
every means to profane our cemetery, deprive
it of its sacred character, and convert it into a
dunghill. We should also be deeply im-
pressed with a strong sense of our duties
toward the resting-place of our dead—duties
that may be summed up in the one word,
Respect. This respect ought to manifest itself
in a fourfold manner; namely, in caring for
the cemetery, and especially the cross; in the

inclosure of the grounds ; in our visits; and in the surroundings of the place.

Our cemeteries, consecrated as they are, and set apart by the Church as receptacles for the remains of God's children, brethren of the Incarnate Word, are, next to our consecrated temples, the holiest spots on earth. Nay more, my dear Frederic, they are so identified with the Church that they are similarly affected. If, for example, the Church should be desecrated, the desecration extends to the soil of the churchyard surrounding; and as it is not lawful to celebrate the holy mysteries in a desecrated church, so too is it wrong to bury in desecrated ground until it be first blessed over again.

Care should be taken of gates and fences so as to prevent cattle from grazing in the grounds. No rubbish, sticks, stones, sweepings of the church, weeds, or other unsightly objects should ever be found within its precincts. The paths should be clean and neat, the headstones kept erect, and the mounds tidily sodded. People should not be permitted to make thoroughfares, much less to hold meetings in these sacred places. The division between the parts consecrated and the unhallowed portion should be scrupulously marked.

Very special attention should be bestowed upon the cross, that image of Him who is the resurrection and the life.

In a well-ordered parish, the cemetery is always carefully inclosed. This is proper; for, as you know, a sleeping man is comparatively defenseless; and the Church watches over us with equal solicitude in our graves and in our cradles. Like the angel with the flaming sword at the gates of paradise, she takes her stand at the cemetery-gate to prevent all intrusion, whether voluntary or involuntary, upon our death-slumbers.

We should make frequent visits to the home of the dead. It is a holy book which speaks most effectively to the eyes of our soul, as well as to those of our body. It speaks thus to rich and poor, young and old: " You will one day be here; I expect you at any moment; for I am the inevitable rendezvous of all generations. Those who are here were once as you are now, and you will soon be just as they are to-day. Do you wish to know what they are, and what you will be? Just lift this stone, dig up a few handfuls of earth, open the coffin, and look!" This will be the end of all your labors, cares, anxieties, and strivings after honors and riches. "Within my womb," it continues, "your body will undergo strange developments, like unto the seed that falls in the furrow from the hand of the husbandman. I am God's field, and you will one day see me covered with a two-fold harvest; one of wheat destined for the granaries of the Master, and another of tares fated to be burned for all ages with the devils in hell. In this place will occur the separation of the sheep from the goats. This will be your starting-point for the valley of Josaphat, to hear pronounced upon you, in presence of assembled nations, that sentence which will decide your lot for all eternity. Here, too, will you catch the first notes of the angel's trumpet, as with power greater than that which shattered the walls of Jericho, it will send its tones into the bowels of the earth, saying, Arise, ye dead, and come to judgment. *Surgite, mortui, venite ad judicium.*" How touching its appeal to our senses! " Saunter through my domain," it says, " and listen to the hundred voices as they issue from the sepulchres. Hear this one say, ' I am your father who labored hard for you;' another, ' I am your mother who once loved you tenderly ;' others again, ' We are your brothers, your sisters, your wife, your husband, your friend, your child, your pastor.'

" Hearken to these voices as, all together, they cry out, ' Have pity on us, O you who were once friends and neighbors! have pity on us now. Remember us when you pray, when you give alms, and at the holy sacrifice of the mass, for Christ died for us all.'"

My dear Frederic, what excellent spiritual reading the cemetery affords! A quarter of an hour given once every week, to this inexhaustible book would convert all men ; for it is written, " In all thy works, remember thy last end, and thou shalt never sin." (Ecclus. 7 : 40.) Yes, our last end—our death, our judgment may be learned in meditation over the graves of the dead. The Church in her motherly solicitude, wishing to have every facility offered to her children, that they may be enabled to study a page of this admirable book at least once a week, when on Sunday they assemble for divine service, places her cemeteries around her altars. To this arrangement, the revolutionists object. Resolved not to permit the cemetery to exist ·near the church, they are just now leaving nothing undone to have it removed out of sight. In this movement they are consistent; for they will thus succeed in utterly destroying every thing that was considered holy, sacred, and moral,

not only among Christians, but even among
the old pagans themselves.

Alas! what will become of our time-honored
devotion toward our dead, if, in order to say
a prayer at their graves, we must undertake a
long and inconvenient journey, with the prospect of finding the gates barred against us,
as is most frequently the case?   Now, a people who forget their dead are ungrateful; and
an ungrateful people are always bad.

As yet, however, notwithstanding the persistent efforts of infidel Communists, the
cemetery is contiguous to the church in most
country Catholic parishes.   This arrangement
is faithfully adhered to in the German portions
of Switzerland.   Neither of us, my dear Frederic, can ever forget the touching sights that
greeted our eyes, at every mile, as we tra-
veled the Cantons of Soleure, Lucerne, and
Schweitz.   In every one of the pretty villages,
you discover a neat church, with its slender
spire, and surrounded by a well-kept cemetery,
whose entrance is also the entrance to the
church.   The gates yield to a gentle pressure of the hand, for they are closed, but
not locked.   You enter upon the well-trim-
med path, and on your left and right you
perceive two elegant pedestals bearing vessels

filled with holy-water, and near them a sprinkler, which you lift to throw a few drops on the nearest graves. The mounds are tidily sodded with greenest turf, and placed in perfectly even rows at equal distances apart. Graveled walks wind their way to each grave, to enable friends to reach with ease and decorum the spot containing the ashes of their loved ones. Every mound has its modest cross about two feet in height, bearing the name, age, and date of death of the deceased, followed by a short prayer, or a quotation from the Holy Scriptures.

When, through the golden haze of an Alpine sunset, you descry in the distance one of these fields of God—as the inhabitants call them—placidly reposing on the mountain-side, with its simple headboards standing range after range in perfectly parallel lines, and painted in colors that contrast beautifully with the brilliant verdure of the graves, a gentle melancholy enters the heart, and as tears start to your eyes, a prayer falls from your lips for the eternal repose of the dead. The memories of former times, of ages of faith, crowd upon us and we are carried back through the long lines of our truly Catholic ancestry, to the Catacombs of Rome.

How striking the resemblance! Here you
have, as in subterranean Rome, the altar of
the principal martyr within the village church,
and around it kneel in pious prayer a group
of Christians preparing for the final struggle.
Surrounding the living you see a cordon of
dead. And although their lips are blanched,
they speak in tones of gentle warning about
detachment from earthly things, of an immortal crown, and of eternal rest. Reluctantly we
leave the scene, but with hearts consoled to
know that our Holy Mother, the Catholic
Church, is ever the same. Our joy would be
full, did not the unwelcome remembrance
break in upon us of a set of men with notions
unworthy of a savage, whose aim it is not only
to shut the dead from the living, but even by
irreligious burial-rites to dishonor our cemeteries, and grant us no better obsequies than
they would give to the horse or mule; an igno-
miny offered only to the unrepentant of the
old law: " He shall be buried with the burial
of an ass, rotten and cast forth, without the
gates of Jerusalem." (Jer. 22 : 19.)

TWELFTH LETTER.

Dear Frederic :

My last letter treated of the reverence and care due to cemeteries, and of the lessons derived from them. "But why," you ask, " are our cemeteries consecrated with so much parade; why sprinkled with holy-water, and perfumed with incense?" Before satisfying your pardonable curiosity, I will give you, in a few brief words, the history of sepulture. Meanwhile, rest assured that our Holy Mother, the Church, does nothing without good and sufficient reasons. The very fact of her saying or doing a thing is evidence enough that it is right and proper.

On going back to remotest pagan antiquity, we find that the resting-places of the dead were within the walls of private dwellings. I will quote only a few authorities. " In early times," says Servius, " the bodies of the dead were kept in their own homes, whence arose the domestic worship of the Lares, and the term, Larvas, given to departed spirits." Another author tells us : " It was the custom among the ancients for each family to preserve its dead in the house. Hence every home had its own worship of 'the *Shades.*'"

We all know that the Egyptians embalmed the bodies of deceased persons, and preserved them carefully at home. People who showed so much love and respect for their dead as not to part with their remains, can not be suspected of sharing the opinions of nineteenth-century Communists, that is, that their respect and love were thrown away on decaying clods of earth. The confused traditional belief in the immortality of the soul, and the consequent faith in the resurrection of the flesh, held at all times and by all nations, is of more weight and importance than all the negations of infidel philosophers.

Of course, respect for the dead, when carried to extremes, degenerated into idolatry ; as is the case with the Chinese to-day in their an-

cestral worship.   History relates that whole
nations of Africa had no other gods than the
" Manes," that is, the spirits of their ancestors.
By them they swore, in their names they consulted the oracles, and by them they were
guided in all affairs of moment.   Indeed,
these practices were becoming so universal
that God, in the Holy Scriptures, decreed
capital punishment against any person found
guilty of consulting departed spirits.   It is,
therefore, many centuries since spiritualism
was condemned.

Sepulture in private houses could never
become very general, or last for any length of
time.   Large as we may suppose the houses
to be, they would soon become too small for
the living and dead.   People soon began to
bury in the temples, thus showing that they
did not despise human remains, as being
naught but decomposing matter.   Nay, history assures us that these temples had their
origin in sepulture; in other words, the first
burial-places were places of worship.   " So
great was the reverence among the ancients
for their tombs that," as Eusebius and Lac-
tantius assert, " they were made the foundations of sacred edifices."

Another writer, describing the funereal

practices of the ancients, says, " Among the people of antiquity, the homes of the dead were held so sacred that they were more scrupulously cared for than the dwellings of the living. They were constantly watched, to guard against profanation by the burial of an unclean stranger, a vicious member of their own community, or by destruction or disturbance of a tomb. It was not allowed to repair a tombstone, if it could not be done without interfering with the ashes of the dead. Every violation was punishable with death, scourging, hard work in the mines, or the amputation of both hands."

The Roman law, therefore, only sanctions a universal custom, when it decrees, " The spot where a man lies buried is sacred." *Ubi corpus de mortui hominis condas, sacer esto.* Ancient reverence naturally gave rise to much extravagance in cemeteries. It knew no bounds among the Romans, as witnessed to-day in Rome, by Adrian's monument, the pyramid of Cestius, and the mausoleum of Cecilia Metella. In Egypt, we have the colossal pyramids of the Pharaohs; whilst in Greece, the extravagance was such, as to call for the enactment of the following law, quoted by Cicero : " On account of the excessive costliness of the tombs erected in the military cemetery at Athens, it is forbidden to put up expensive structures, or those requiring more than eight days in their construction. No statuary must be set up, and no discourse is to be delivered except by the public officer whose duty it is to do so."

If pagans thus honored their dead, we must not wonder at the respect paid by the Church, in all ages, to her holy martyrs. Although the early Christians were generally poor, yet they cheerfully sacrificed their all to beautify the resting-places of those heroic witnesses of the faith. Marble, porphyry, bronze, silver, and gold were all employed to prepare worthy receptacles for their consecrated ashes.

Long after the dispersion at Babel, the nations preserved a dim recollection of the sentence pronounced by God against their first father, "Dust thou art, and unto dust thou shalt return," (Gen. 3 : 19,) and scrupulously laid their dead in the earth. Cremation, or the burning of bodies, practiced by the Romans, Greeks, Gauls, and Germans, comes at a much later period. Its origin, according to the elder Pliny, was as follows : " The early Romans did not consume their dead ; but finding by experience in later years, that the bodies of soldiers killed in battle and buried in distant lands were afterward dug up by the enemy, it was decided, thereafter, to burn these bodies on the battle-field, and carry away the ashes. Inhumation, however, was always more or less practiced. Thus, no member of the Cornelia family was ever burned prior to the time of Sylla, the dictator; and he wished to have his body consumed on the funeral pile, lest it should be dug up and mutilated by the friends of Marius, whose body he himself had thus treated." The practice of burning the dead was discontinued under Constantine.

At no period of their history, even when cremation was universally practiced, did the Romans lose sight of the fitness of burial in the earth. Cicero is very clear on this matter, when he tells us, " Previous to the earth being thrown upon the dead, the place where the body has been burned is not held sacred ; but when the earth has been cast upon the dead they are considered buried, and the place then enjoys many sacred privileges." Horace and Virgil both allude to this belief. " Throw upon my body, " says the first, "a few handfuls of earth, and then go thy way." Virgil says, " Throw earth upon my remains." It was a sacred duty for every traveler to stop, and throw some earth upon any lifeless body which he might meet lying unburied. The dead were supposed to beg this act of mercy. Seneca assures us that this law of charity was considered more binding than any written in the code. Whence arose this desire of having the dead covered with earth? From a confused remembrance of the right method of burial, as ordered by God, when He condemned man to death; as well as from the superstitious yet common belief among pagans, that the soul of an unburied corpse was condemned to wander up and down the banks of the river Styx, for one hundred years. To this kind of purgatory, or non-interment, pagan law condemned parricides, matricides, and suicides. The last had their hands cut off, and thrown into the common sink. The Hebrews left their suicides above ground. The Athenians amputated the guilty hand, and buried it apart from the body. In our enlightened age, in which suicide abounds, all these salutary penalties, which were so many wholesome protestations of society against the worst of crimes, have been abolished. Where are we going to stop?

THIRTEENTH LETTER.

CREMATION—WHY PRACTICED—MODE OF SAVING THE ASHES—
ANCIENT "COLUMBARIES" — GENERAL CEMETERIES—THEIR
ANTIQUITY—THE PROPERTY OF THE CHURCH.

MY DEAR FRIEND:

Society has practiced two kinds of sepulture; inhumation and cremation. I have already spoken of inhumation or burial under
ground. Why was cremation practiced, and
how were the ashes of the corpse distinguished
from the ashes of the funeral pile? These
two questions I will now answer.

In the first place, what was the process in
burning bodies? The obsequies of the
wealthy inhabitants of Rome were performed
in the Field of Mars, where funeral piles, in
the shape of altars, were erected, and tastefully
and richly ornamented. On one of these, the
body, sprinkled with perfumes, was carefully
laid, with its face toward heaven. Then the
nearest relative, holding a lighted torch be-

hind him, walked backward to the pile, and set it on fire. As it was believed that the spirit of the deceased person was pleased with the shedding of blood, oxen and sheep were slaughtered and thrown into the flames. For the same reason, gladiators fought before the pile while the fire was burning. These combats were a substitute for the more ancient cruel practice of immolating prisoners of war near the funeral piles of soldiers slain in battle.

As soon as the body was consumed, the fire was quenched with wine; the ashes and charred bones gathered up, washed in milk and wine, and then inclosed in an urn, sometimes of great value.

Such was the cremation of the rich. That of the poor and the slaves was carried out with much less ceremony. Their bodies were thrown indiscriminately into large pits surrounded with high walls, and in which burned large quantities of resinous wood. These were on the Esquiline hill, without the city. It was by special privilege, that even the rich had their obsequies within the walls, and in the public square; for a law of the twelve tables forbade their performance within the city limits. *In urbe ne sepelito neque urito.*

Now that you are aware of the practice of

burning the dead, you may wish to know the reasons for it. Although I have consulted very many learned writers, both living and dead, on this point, I have not found any satisfactory answer. Some, quoting Pliny, pretend that the bodies were burned to secure them against profanation. This was very well as regards the bodies of soldiers dying far away from home and in an enemy's country; but it does not explain the common practice of burning the people of the city of Rome, where no profanation need be apprehended. Neither does it explain cremation among the Greeks, Germans, and Gauls.

There are some who claim, that the bodies were burned to save them from a slower and sadder decomposition by worms and serpents in the earth; as well also that the relatives might have the comfort of having near them an everlasting portion of those whom they had loved when alive. In any case, it can not be said, that contempt or dislike had any thing to do with this custom.

There are many who pretend to discover an inspiration of the devil in the practice. For in the first place, cremation did not come into use, until inhumation had been practiced for centuries; and even then it was confined

to certain localities. It is extremely repug-
nant to our feelings of love toward the bodies
of our friends, to have them crisped and charred. It is evidently not of divine inspiration;
for it is the very opposite of inhumation as
regulated by the primitive sentence of God
Himself. It is opposed to the practice of the
people of God, and to all very ancient peoples generally. It is opposed to the spirit of
Christianity, which, considering the custom a
cruel and barbarous one, never practiced it;
nay, sought the earliest opportunity, under
Constantine, to abolish it.

In a word, God has said, " The body of
man will return to the earth whence it came,
there to be transformed, in order to rise again
immortal." God's eternal adversary, the devil,
would reply, " It must not be as you say;
man must be burnt; for in thus annihilating
him as much as possible, I will wipe out all
knowledge of, and belief in, the dogma of the
resurrection." He succeeded but too well; if
we may believe Tertullian, whose words I will
quote in confirmation of the above. " The
ignorant laugh at our ideas of a resurrection,
and say that nothing remains of us after
death. And yet they continually pay homage
to their dead by great and costly parades,

sumptuous banquets, which they claim are
pleasing to those dead in whom they refuse to
admit any life, feeling, or knowledge. I, in
my turn, and with good reason, laugh at these
people, who after they have barbarously charred and crisped their dead, then feed them,
and in the same moment honor and insult
them by fire.   Piety playing with cruelty.   Is
it an honor or an insult to burn articles of
food for those whom they are burning?"   If
we want any further evidence that cremation
is an inspiration of the devil, we have only to
listen to the preachings of our modern pagans
in France and Italy, who clamor for a return
to this detestable practice of antiquity.

We will now examine the mode whereby
the human ashes were distinguishable from
those of the wood and animals consumed in
the same fire.   Here, also, the learned have
not much to say.   It is quite certain, however, that the ancients had some means of
knowing one from the other.   What was it?
Well, the most probable opinion is, that in
the centre of the top of the pile there was set
an iron or brick oven in which the body was
burned without permitting the ashes to scat-
ter, or allowing the other ashes to get mixed
with them.   The practice of burning bodies

and saving their ashes gave rise to a sort of cemetery called a columbary. This name took its origin from the little openings, like pigeon-holes, made in the wall, and in which the urns holding the ashes were set. Each of these openings was closed with a slab bearing on its outer surface, the name of the person whose remains were within. In common with most Roman tourists, you and I have visited the columbaries of Hylas, and of the freedmen of Augustus. They are large square chambers excavated in the earth, whose entrance is by an easy stair-way hewn in the rock. Although these columbaries were not cemeteries in the true sense of the word, yet they prove that the custom of keeping and owning a place of burial for the use of a community, a corporation, or a family is as old as the world itself. Whilst, as regards cemeteries in the correct and proper sense of the word, nothing is more evident. For the Scriptures tell us that the patriarch Abraham, not owning any land, purchased a cave in the vale of Mambre, which he fitted up as a family vault, buried in it his wife Sarah, and was buried there himself, as were his descendants, Jacob and Joseph. The Israelites esteemed it a blessing to be interred near

their fathers, and a greater misfortune could
hardly befall them than to be excluded from
the tombs of their ancestors. This exclusion
was one of the most dreaded threats made by
God to the guilty.

The pagans, too, even those who burned
their dead, had places of general sepulture.
Witness, besides the columbary lately describ-
ed, the necropolis of Egypt and of Athens.
In Pompeii, the cemetery is found to be at
the entrance to the city. In your visits to the
capital of the world, you must have noticed
the long lines of tombs bordering the Appian
Way. Every traveler has stopped to gaze
upon the mausoleums of Cestius and Cecilia
Metella, and penetrate into the mortuary
chamber of the Scipios. Like Abraham, the
wealthy Romans purchased plots of ground
to form the resting-places of their bones and
those of their family after death.

The Turks have their cemeteries, which
they hold to be as sacred as did the ancient
Greeks and Romans their burial-places.
They visit them, too, and in lieu of prayers,
have the Mussulman priests to read, from the
Koran, passages expressive of respect for the
dead.

The Christians, of course, always had their

cemeteries. After being kept for three centuries under ground, as soon as persecutions ceased, the Church placed her cemeteries in the sunshine. So they have continued. They were her property, because they were sacred places, and blessed with her blessings. It is eminently right and proper that the mother should have full control of the dormitory where her children sleep.

In my next, I will reply to your question, Why does the Church bless cemeteries ?

FOURTEENTH LETTER.

MY DEAR FRIEND:

I now reply to your question, Why does the Church bless cemeteries? For various reasons: among others to proclaim her faith in the sanctity of the human body, in the dogma of universal charity, and in our glorious destiny beyond the grave. Consequently she blesses them, first to save them from all profane uses, to expel the spirits of darkness, and to intrust them to the care of the angels: secondly, to bear witness that the faithful, whose bodies lie here buried, died within her communion, and belong, as far as she can judge, to the society of the elect. By this blessing, the cemetery becomes, for the faithful departed, a sort of subterranean church where they are awaiting a glorious

138

resurrection. Thirdly, the Church blesses cemeteries to testify to her children her motherly affection, by following them even into the grave, and beyond it. By her example she moves us to works of mercy, so lauded in the Scriptures, where we are commanded to procure for the dead honorable sepulture. She reminds us of the pious Tobias, and imitates the holy women who cared for the tomb of Our Saviour. Fourthly, the Church blesses cemeteries to make them a place of prayer for the use of the faithful living, and to invite all Christians to pray for their dead brethren. This blessing not only sanctifies the ground where the deceased faithful are to lie, but it is advantageous to their souls. It remains attached to the very soil, like a continual prayer, in which the Church invokes divine mercy in favor of the faithful departed, that at the last day they may hear the angel's trumpet to their glory and happiness.

See, then, the immense advantage of sepulture in consecrated ground; and what cruelty it is to deny it to the dead. How justly may be applied to the Communists the words of Holy Scripture, " The bowels of the wicked are cruel." (Prov. 12 : 10.) Place yourself in front of one of those fearful volcanoes of man's

industry, a burning furnace.   Imagine you see
your wife, or child, or some dear friend, falling
into the yawning gulf of fire.   You have it in
your power to save the victim, but an officer
of the law or a deputation from an enlightened society endeavors to thwart your efforts
telling you that to save them would be only
superstition.   Where is the man that would
listen to such nonsense, or submit to such
tyranny?   To fight against such interference
would be a solemn duty.

As already stated, the Church blesses her
cemeteries in order to manifest her respect for
the bodies of the faithful, her faith in the
dogma of universal brotherhood, as well as in
our glorious destiny beyond the tomb.   Here
begins the real subject of this and my subsequent letters.   In our time, no subject is
more important.   Pray, then, to God and His
Blessed Mother that I may prove equal to the
task which friendship for you has imposed
upon me.

The cemetery is a most eloquent preacher
on the sanctity of man's body in general, and
especially of the body of the Christian.   " I
am sanctified," it says, " I am a consecrated
vessel, a reliquary; for I am set apart to
receive something holy, namely, your body."

In fact, next to the soul, nothing is nobler or holier than your flesh. To understand this truth, hear what Tertullian — that eloquent doctor, who has been the admiration of ages— says :

" The first and chief claim which your body has to love and respect is founded in the great majesty of its Creator ; for it was made not by a man nor by an angel, but by God Himself. The difference between God's manner of making man and other creatures is vast. To call the latter into existence, a word was sufficient ; but for man's creation, God used not only His word, but his hand. Yes, God's hand was used to establish man's sovereignty, so as not to confound him with other creatures : He *formed* him—*finxit hominem.*

" At the more sound of God's voice all the inferior creatures sprang into existence, and at once became man's servants. Whilst in order to make man the king of creation, he was fashioned by the divine hand. This is a sign of royalty. Remember that man is properly termed flesh, and this was his first name. 'The Lord God formed man of the slime of the earth.' (Gen. 2 : 7.) Already man, and yet slime of the earth, *jam homo qui adhuc limus.* 'And God . . . breathed into his face the breath of life.' (Gen. 2 : 7.) Thus man, as yet the slime of the earth, becomes complete —*adeo homo figmentum primò, dehinc totus.* In this I wish to show and teach man that what God has done for him is due not exclusively to his soul, but also to his body—*non soli animæ, verum et carni, scias debitum.*"*

Thus the chief source of our body's nobility and its first claim to our respect is the fact of its being God's work. But there is a second claim, more sacred than the first. For our body is formed after the model of that of the Word made flesh. Hear Tertullian again : " In the construction of this body, a great thing has been accomplished; for every time that it was touched by the hand of God— each time that it was divided, cut, extended, fashioned—so each time it was specially honored. Do you not see God intently engaged in this work? using His hand with jealous care, His thought, His labor, His deliberation, His wisdom, His providence, and especially His love in forming its parts?"

And why all this painstaking on the part of the Creator? Because He had uppermost in His mind, while making man, the thought of Christ, the future perfect Man. The Word

---

* De Resurrect. Carnis, c. v.

which was with God, and which was God, was in future time, when becoming man, to assume this carefully-fashioned slime of the earth. This human nature, which the Creator was now forming with such extreme care, was to be united with the Divine nature in the one person of Jesus Christ, and placed at the right hand of God the Father. Hence humanity was even more than the likeness of God. *Non tantum opus Dei erat, sed et pignus*—it was not only God's work, but a pledge of God's love. Of what account, then, are the sneers of the infidel who affects to despise his body? Let him remember the power and majesty of its great Creator, who deemed slime of the earth a fit subject for the display of His greatest attributes.

God breathed the breath of life, an immortal soul, into this body of man. Yes, the human body becomes the tabernacle of God's breathing. Tertullian thus describes this mystery: " The lifeless clay becomes glorious and beautiful under the influence of the Creator's breathing. The rough stone is now a brilliant diamond. Man invents costly vessels to hold his rare wines, artistic caskets to contain his jewels, elaborate scabbards to protect the sensitive steel of his valuable sword. Would

God imprison a soul, His own image, His own
breath, in a senseless, shapeless coffin? No:
He consigned it to a well-constructed body.
He united the two so closely that it is difficult
to know whether the flesh leads the spirit, or
the spirit leads the flesh; whether the soul
obeys the body, or the body obeys the soul.
While it is of faith that the soul asserts authority over the body, and gives it character and
motion, as being nearer to the Divinity, to the
body belongs the honor and glory of containing the soul, and sharing its power.

" What is there of all the beauty and wealth
of the world that is not enjoyed by the soul
through the instrumentality of the body? By
the agency of the flesh, the soul enjoys the
sense of sight, hearing, and touch. Through
the body it receives its communications from
heaven, and gives its homage to God. If
body and soul are so necessary to each other
here below, why not in heaven, in order to
attain to a full complement of happiness?"

The human body, then, is a work of God,
an expression of His wisdom and love; is formed after the divine model of the Word made
flesh. It is the sanctuary of the soul, shares
its power, and is the necessary medium of

its joys. What more noble than this body of ours?

Be not surprised, my dear Frederic, that I thus dwell at length upon the truths suggested by our treatise on sepulture. When was it ever more necessary to remind man of his own dignity? We live in an age when men treat their persons as if they were clods of earth turned up by the plow. Though some there are, too, who claim the duty of rehabilitating the flesh. What sacrilege is this? Rehabilitation of the flesh, as they understand it, is its degradation, defilement, and profanation. They would rehabilitate the body by degrading and defiling it with the virus of concupiscence. To enable it to enjoy, as they say, more fully the gratification of its basest desires, they pretend to develop and strengthen it by excess of eating and drinking, by idleness, unlawful pleasures, and countless nameless acts of iniquity.

It is not in this way that God would have us show our respect for our body, that masterpiece of His hand, the image of His Divine Son, the sanctuary of an immortal soul. The proper way to respect our body is to make it subservient to the end for which

God made it; to esteem it as sacred as the vessels on the altar, to discipline it so as to render it strong and healthy, by the practice of temperance in all things. This indispensable duty is too often neglected.

FIFTEENTH LETTER.

MY DEAR FRIEND:

Of all created beings, the most noble and beautiful are, beyond all question, the angels and the souls of men. Next to them stands the human body. And if the bodies of all men are deserving of our respect, even those of pagans and unregenerated savages, what shall we say of the eminent sanctity of the Christian's body? The body of the unbaptized heathen is a figure more or less deformed of the Word made flesh; the sanctuary of an unregenerated soul, and the co-worker of this soul, although only in deeds of the purely natural order. Such is the three-fold glory of the pagan's body. But this glory belongs to the Christian in an eminent degree.

A soul purified by the waters of Baptism is endowed with a superhuman beauty which

147

shines out through its body, and which is preserved in that body till tarnished by the first
sin. Hence the fact, admitted by observing
·men, that the true type of genuine beauty is
found among Christians only; among Christians in Catholics, and among Catholics in
the angelic youth, or the virginal maiden.
Missionaries assure us that the reception of
baptism by the savage and cannibal so chan-
ges and improves the expression of countenance that they are hardly recognizable. This
beauty is one source of glory for the Christian's body and one claim to our respect.

The Christian's body, unlike that of the
heathen, is the sanctuary or tabernacle, not
of a sin-stained soul, of a soul without beauty
in the eyes of God, but the tabernacle of a
soul whose beauty rivals that of the angels,
eclipses that of all visible creatures, of a beauty which while it ravishes the heart of God
Himself, becomes a bright mirror in which He
loves to contemplate His own incomparable
perfections. Nay, my dear friend, in holy
Communion, this same body becomes the tabernacle of God Himself in person. What
more can be said in its favor? This is the
second source of the body's glory, and another title to our respect.

There is still another, and greater if possible. The Christian body is the associate of the soul in all works of the supernatural order. To appreciate the dignity to which the body is entitled by reason of this sublime and mysterious coöperation with the soul, suffice it to say with Tertullian that the body is the pivot of eternal salvation, and so necessary that the soul could not be united to God, without its coöperation. The body is washed in baptism, that the soul may be cleansed. The body is anointed, that the soul may be consecrated. The body receives imposition of hands, that the soul may be illumined by the Holy Spirit. The body is fed with the Holy Eucharist, that the soul may be strengthened in grace. The body and soul, one in their labors, can not be separated in their rewards.

How would mortification of soul, fastings, and all kinds of austerity, those sacrifices so pleasing to God, be possible without the painful coöperation of the body? Is it not from attributes of the body that the fragrant incense of virginity, holy widowhood, and chaste wedlock takes its rise?

What must be our admiration of the Christian's body when, in defense of faith, it is made the object of men's hatred, cast into prison, horribly maltreated, dragged to the scene of execution, striving in its death-agony to imitate its Saviour, and finally dying a most excruciating death? Is not the Christian body happy and glorious, nay, highly privileged in thus faithfully discharging a sublime duty, in the very act of discharging which it renders to God all that He desires—a pure soul, at the same moment ending all its own sufferings?

From all this, my dear Frederic, you may form some idea of a Christian body, and of its high and noble duties. You will learn every day more fully to appreciate these truths, if you bear in mind that God by uniting our flesh to our soul, has identified it necessarily with religion. This He has effected in so admirable a manner that, if the soul be deprived of its freedom to manifest its love by using the tongue, hands, and prostrations of the body, it is deprived of its most consoling means of the worship that it would fain render to God. But if the soul, when inwardly moved, be free to act upon the body, raising its eyes to heaven, extending its hands, bending its knees and manifesting its adoration in many ways, with hymns, and sighs, and tears of joy or repentance, the heart is relieved and comforted. It would seem that it is not so much the soul associating the body to its piety and devotion, as the body hastening to the soul's aid. In our most spiritual act, that of receiving communion, the body ministers to the soul, and becomes the instrument through which it receives the sacrament. In martyrdom, too, the body is the visible witness, defender, and sufferer. This is a third glory of the Christian body, its third claim to our respect.

Need we be astonished, then, my dear friend, at St. Paul's counsel to Christians, that they respect their bodies? " Glorify," he says, "and bear God in your bodies. You are temples of the Holy Ghost, and members of Jesus Christ. Woe to him who defiles his flesh, for he defiles the temple of God; and God will destroy him who profaneth His temple." Need we wonder that the Church honors the body, even after death, with profound respect? I say the Church; because it is from her faithfully preserved store of traditions that we draw and enjoy these manifestations of gladness and reverence in regard to the Christian body.

It has always been the custom, from earliest times, to gently close the eyes of deceased persons, that the countenance may bear a

calm and tranquil expression. Attendants always carefully washed the remains of recently
departed friends ; for a body so often sanctified
in life, should return to the bosom of its mother earth cleansed from every stain. Among
many instances of this practice we have that of
Charlemagne, the great Christian emperor.
Indeed, it was looked upon as a great misfortune to be buried without this purification.
When practicable, the body was embalmed in
imitation of Our Lord, wrapped up in a white
linen sheet and other stuffs more or less costly.
St. Jerome tells us that devotedness to the
dead sometimes exceeded the bounds of Christian moderation. Yet when confined within
just limits, especially in the case of persons
representing God, the Church never found
fault.

Let me mention some other modes of
showing respect to human remains, and they
will prove, more and more fully, that the way
our ancestors had of treating their dead was
the very opposite to that of the infidels.
The body, placed in the coffin, was exposed
at the door of the house. This custom,
which existed among the Greeks and Romans, is still followed by the Parisians. As
you pass by the dwelling where death has

entered, you perceive in the porch, a small chapel in which, surrounded by lighted tapers, lies the coffin with the never-forgotten vessel of holy-water by its side. Ancient liturgists thus explain this custom which has for centuries been a very important part of a Parisian's religion. " The remains of the dead are thus exposed, in order to warn the heedless passers-by of the uncertainty of life and the certainty of death, and also to implore their pious prayers for the faithful departed." It is but fair to add that no one, not even an "*enlightened animal*," passes the chapel or meets a funeral without sprinkling holy-water, making the sign of the cross, or at least lifting the hat. Another custom, equally ancient in the Church, is to always place the bodies of deceased persons in coffins made of wood. St. Ambrose tells us that this custom is indicative of hope in a future resurrection ; for although wood had previously no special signification, it became from the time that our Lord used it in His crucifixion in order to conquer death, a symbol of life. I will mention in conclusion but two other customs. The members of some religious orders bury their dead in a bed of flowers, and I know a community of nuns, founded as early

as the sixth century, whose rule and custom
it is to reverently kiss the feet of a deceased
sister, before consigning her remains to the
grave. It is unnecessary to add that all these
practices still exist in truly Christian countries, and that it is much to be desired to see
them reëstablished wherever they have fallen
into disuse.

Coming back to the cemetery question, I
ask ; Is it to be wondered at, that the Church
uses so much solemnity in blessing the place
where Christian bodies are to rest ? No, my
dear friend, we should not be astonished at
that, but we may well be astonished, confound-
ed, grieved, and overwhelmed with distress, at
seeing the great want of respect among the
living, for their own bodies, and how easily
and carelessly men who are slaves of passion,
defile and profane their own or those of their
fellow-creatures. In fear and trembling, I
would recall to their minds these divine
words : " Man, when he was in honor, did not
understand : he is compared to senseless
beasts, and is become like to them." I fear
for their salvation, for God will not fail to punish the desecrators of His temples : " But if
any man violate the temple of God, him shall
God destroy," says St. Paul. (I. Cor. 3 : 17.)

SIXTEENTH LETTER.

One more Reason why the Church blesses her Cemeteries—Second Sermon preached by the Cemetery :
Doctrine of Universal Brotherhood—Interments
within Church Edifices—Words of St. Chrysostom.

My Dear Friend :

In our day of gross sensuality, man is rapidly losing sight of the respect due to his body.
In the hope of awakening him to a sense of
duty on this essential point of Christian, social, and physical life, I will adduce one
more reason why the Church blesses her cemeteries; and one which, while including all
the preceding, displays most brilliantly the
faith of our holy mother, the Church, and her
profound respect for the bodies of her children.

She blesses her cemeteries, then, to manifest her respect for the bodies of the faithful;
bodies which the Apostle Paul calls temples of the Holy Ghost, and members of Jesus

155

Christ.   These members having been sanctified and dedicated to God in baptism, by holy anointings and by the Blessed Eucharist, it is right and proper that they should be laid in holy ground.   If, in obedience to the sentence pronounced by God against disobedient creatures, they must return to dust, it is only to await a glorious resurrection to a better existence in heaven.   They belong to souls who are already enjoying the beatific vision of God in the city of the saints.

It is true the Church places upon her altars for our veneration, the relics of those only, whose holiness of life has been fully proved by miracles.   Still, the bodies of those faithful who have died in the state of grace, and consequently are destined to attain certain glory in heaven, doubtless have a share in that veneration which we pay to the precious remains of God's servants, and may, in a certain sense, be termed " sacred relics."   Their resting-place, therefore, ought to be holy.

Now, my dear Frederic, recall to mind my preceding letters, and tell me are we not justified in having our cemeteries blessed? Tell me, too, whether there is any other more eloquent mode, than that employed by the cemetery of proclaiming the sanctity of our body, or of more successfully refuting the degrading doctrines of the infidels, according to whom we are but lumps of earth.

Let us now hear the second sermon that the cemetery preaches; " On the doctrine of universal and eternal brotherhood."

On this subject, our great preacher is equally successful. His pulpit and his subject are closely identified—indeed, they are both one and the same thing. Does death sever all ties between those who have departed from this life, and those who yet remain? Nature answers, Yes: faith says, No, and says it by the voice of the cemetery. In order that all, young and old, rich and poor, may hear this voice, the cemetery is placed near the church. Here, owing to its very position, it talks to us night and day on the consoling doctrine of the communion of saints; a doctrine as universal and as ancient as Christianity itself. In thus placing our tomb and our cradle side by side, the Church succeeds in making us think of the dead, and in helping them by our prayers; as also in making us profit by the lessons which they give forth in solemn silence; in a word, she keeps the living and the dead in close contact, so that we may minister to their relief, and they may contri-

bute to our encouragement and consolation.
Let me develop this thought in a few words.
The cemetery is situated close to the church,
in order that we may not forget the dead, or
be ourselves forgotten by those who will survive us.   In order to discharge the important
duty of praying for the dead, we must first
think about them.   Just to effect this remembrance, and to make it continual, the cemetery
is always near the spot where the whole parish assembles on Sundays and holy days. Remove the cemetery out of sight, and what will
be the result?   As I have already said, the
dead will be speedily forgotten.

Now, it is a bad sign for parish, family, or
child to forget its dead.   This forgetfulness is
base ingratitude, for we are indebted to our
dead for many things, even for life itself.   It
is a misfortune for ourselves ; for the memory
of departed friends often becomes the foundation of a spiritual fortune for the living.   How
frequently do the last words of an expiring father, or the dying admonition of a loving and
beloved mother become to us a beacon-light
to guide us safely through the journey of life !
I appeal, my dear friend, to your own experience.   Is there any thing that we would more
speedily lose than the memories of our depart-

ed brethren, were they not buried in a place where we may see their graves every time we go to worship God? Take them out of our sight, and in vain will the poor souls cry out in their loneliness, " Have pity on us, have pity, you who were once our friends and neighbors."

As a just retribution, God will permit us to be treated as we have treated others. If we forget our departed brethren, we in our turn will be forgotten by those who survive us. No prayer will be uttered over our grave to shorten our time of suffering. No tear will fall upon its turf to cool the flames of purgatory.

The cemetery is placed near the church, moreover, to give lessons of wisdom to the living. What better preparation for the worship of God on Sunday, than to pass near the dead on our way to the house of prayer? The very sight of this small portion of the earth, where rich and poor lie side by side; where we see the mounds heaving upon the bosoms of our friends and relations; the sight of the spot where we shall one day be laid, must all necessarily give rise in our hearts to serious thought. Now, serious thought is akin to pious thought, and pious thought is the life and soul of prayer.

It is thus that the cemetery, when adjoining the church, constantly preaches the doctrine of universal and everlasting brotherhood: " Living and dead, you are still but one family." The Church upon earth and the Church in purgatory can not be separated by the hand of death. The most intimate and tender relations will continue to bind them together, till the dawning of that day on which, united in each other's embrace, they will both be merged into the Church triumphant.

The Church has been extremely solicitous to keep alive this doctrine of universal brotherhood, of true Christian charity, among members of the human family. Looking upon it as the foundation of Christianity, the keystone in the arch of human society, the principle of all virtue, she has set it up before the eyes of our soul as well as of our body, by her practice of joining the cemetery with the church. Her intention was always plain to her children, and they responded faithfully. You know that the earliest Christian burials took place in the galleries and chapels of the catacombs, where divine service was held.

It was a source of great comfort to our worthy ancestors to know that, after death, they would rest near the holy martyrs, or better yet, near the Holy of Holies each day descending upon the altar, or perhaps remaining there continually in the Blessed Sacrament. To be in such blessed company was considered by the early Christians a bond of charity and a safe protection against evil spirits, whilst at the same time it gratified their tender affections toward those whom they had loved in life. "Lovely and comely in their life, even in death they were not divided." (II. Kings 1 : 23.)

The Church did not forget, in the days of her prosperity, her pious practices during the first three centuries of poverty and persecution. Her children, faithful imitators of their zealous fathers, continued to bury their deceased brethren near the churches, and sometimes within them. The practice of burying within the sacred edifices was, however, discontinued at an early day, especially among the Orientals. Thus, Constantine was not buried within the walls, but in the porch of the Basilica of Saints Peter and Paul. At which St. Chrysostom remarked, " Emperors discharge, in the home of the sinner, the duties discharged by the porters in the palace of the Cæsars."*

---

*Quod Christus sit Deus, n. 9, p. 697, opp., and I. Pars altera, edit. Gaume.

In the West, too, interments in churches were generally prohibited, although exceptions were occasionally made in favor of bishops, abbots, distinguished members of the higher clergy, princes, and founders of churches.[*] Little by little, the primitive practice was revived; so after some years no distinction was made.   Rome herself set the example of burying all classes of Christians, who had died in her communion, in the churches; and her eldest daughter, France, faithfully followed in her footsteps, down to the period of the revolution, in the last century.   Where the churches, cloisters, and chapels were not ample enough to receive all the population, care was taken to gratify the desire of the faithful, by providing grounds as near the church as possible, and devoting them to burial purposes.

In the early ages of Christianity, as the pagan towns but recently converted to Christianity had no room near their temples for the purpose, cemeteries were established near the approaches to the towns.   This fact we learn from St. Chrysostom, who informs us that " The tombs or monuments of the dead stand on the roadside, near the entrance

[*] Conc. de Mayence, 813. c. 55 ; de Meaux, 845, c. 72.

to the cities, like teachers of humility and preachers on human littleness. The traveler just before entering a proud city, where the great and the wealthy of this world live in luxury, meets, at the gates, this grim monitor, warning him of his future dissolution, and then proceeds to visit the wonders of the town."*

We shall see in our next letter how this practice fell into disuse.

---

* Ecloga de Morte, et alibi, De Fide et Lege.

SEVENTEENTH LETTER.

My Dear Friend :

I have already stated that the custom of
burying at the entrance to the towns was not
of long duration, at least among Christians.
In the first place, the towns, growing, soon took
these burial-places within their boundaries;
and besides, pieces of land were secured near
the churches by purchase or donation, and in
these were laid the bodies of the faithful departed. Thenceforward, the cemeteries were
public and above ground.

I doubt whether a single city or town, built
in Europe during the past fifteen hundred
years, had not its cemetery near the church,

or, as in Rome and France, in the vaults beneath. There were several celebrated cemeteries in Paris; among others, " The Holy Innocents," " St. Sulpice," and " St. Médard," while her catacombs contain millions of mortal remains, so that, in making excavations, bones are met in every quarter. This fact will not surprise you ; for you know that around every new church which was built, a large tract of land was set apart and used for the interment of the congregation attending it. I would add that these grounds were held to be so sacred that they served and were recognized as *Sanctuaries*, or places of refuge into which the civil law dare not follow the criminal.

A celebrated council held at Rome under Pope Nicholas II., in 1059, directs that about two hundred feet square be set apart near each large church, and half that space near every smaller one, to receive the bodies of the deceased members of the congregation. After asserting that this practice was followed by the fathers in very early times, it threatens with excommunication any one presuming to violate these holy places.*   As a result of this council's decree, you will find, that there is not an old parish-church in Europe to-day,

---

* Apud Hard. Act. Conc. vi. 1058.

without its contiguous cemetery. And it is this venerable institution that modern impiety seeks to destroy!

The origin of blessing cemeteries dates back to the dim twilight of Christianity. It is at least as old as church-consecration, from which it takes its rise. Canon law has ever taught that the cemetery adjacent to the church is consecrated by the consecration of the church itself. This seems quite natural; for in consecrating the church, many outside benedictions and sprinklings are performed over the exterior walls and the grounds on which the building is reared.*

If, in some exceptional case, the cemetery was detached and distant from the church, recourse was had to a separate consecration. We find an instance of this in the sixth century. The abbess of a convent in Poitiers, having been deputed to superintend the obsequies of Radegunda, Queen of France, anxiously inquires how she is to discharge her duty properly, if the bishop, who was absent, could not get back in time to consecrate the burial-place which had not even been blessed.†

---

* Mand. de Monseignor Malou, Bishop of Bruges.
† Greg. Tur. De Gloria Confess. c. cvi.

The cemetery also teaches a common broth-erhood through the rites and ceremonies to be performed before we are admitted into its pre-cincts, and also by its manner of receiving us. If, as the "solidaires" pretend, man were but a soulless clod of earth, and his corpse a mere mass of vile matter in a state of decomposi-tion, it should be thrown without delay into some sewer or sink. But such is not the be-lief of the human race. See, my dear friend, what takes place among Catholics, who, you know, are just as virtuous and enlightened as any other people, if not more so. As soon as death has seized a member, a marked mani-festation of the indissoluble union between living and dead immediately takes place in a variety of ways. No sooner is the person dead, than his body becomes sacred. A brother has left us, but he is not annihilated. He is approached in religious silence. Night and day, persons watch in prayer around the cof-fin. When it is time to carry him to the church, it is the priest who gives the order of removal, and then precedes the corpse to the foot of the altar. Relations, friends, and neighbors follow in solemn procession, with prayer and hymn, sighs and tears. The Church then employs the mysterious pomp of most expressive ceremony, as well to honor the dead as to instruct the living.

You know, my dear friend, that these mysterious ceremonies, which were abolished by Protestants, are of venerable antiquity, dating back to the beginning of Christianity. Before proving this truth, I shall say a few words about carrying the corpse, and one or two about the catafalque.

It is customary now, especially in the cities, to have the body carried in a hearse ; like so much merchandise or freight on a cart. This custom was not known to our forefathers. They looked upon it as an honor and a work of mercy to render this last service of carrying a deceased friend. The example of Tobias, who was so highly praised in Holy Scripture, and so handsomely rewarded, gave rise to, and encouraged, this pious custom. So strictly was it observed that the body of St. Bruno, Archbishop of Cologne, was carried in this way, by hand, from Rheims to Cologne, a journey of eight full days.* It was by rare exception that a corpse was transported on wheels. Would that it were ever so ! As an evidence that the pious customs of a Catholic people can not be entirely and at once oblite-

* In Vit. apud Surium, 11 Octob.

rated, a vestige of the ancient mode of carrying a corpse may be seen in the present fashion, whose meaning but few understand, of
the mourners holding cords and tassels de-
pending from the hearse.

The catafalque, or *castrum doloris*, perpe-
tuates another traditionary usage. This
empty tomb, into which the coffin is put during the divine office, is a memento of the custom of burying in the churches. The large
white cross, worked upon the black pall, is an
emblem of hope in immortality amid the very
gloom of death.*

I shall now speak of the antiquity of our
funeral service. " How far from the true and
beautiful," says the learned Duranti, " are those
who despise and reject our funeral rites!
From the foundation of Christianity, our ancestors have taught us how to bury the bodies
of Christians with uniform ceremony, and to
embellish their obsequies with every mark of
respect ; for these bodies have been the home
of immortal souls."†

Pope St. Clement orders that the dead be
carefully buried, their obsequies respectfully
performed, and alms distributed in their

---

* Encyclop. Théol. v. Sepulture.
† De Rit. etc. p. 182.

name.* " We have been taught," says Origen,
"to honor the soul gifted with reason, by consigning honorably to its grave the body which
had served it."†

St. Jerome adds, " We need not wonder that
the obsequies of Moses and Aaron were celebrated, according to ancient custom, with
much pomp of ceremony ; for we behold, in
the full light of the Gospel, as recorded in the
Acts of the Apostles, the brethren of Jerusalem giving orders for St. Stephen's funeral,
and making ' great mourning over him.' You
may be sure that this great mourning consist-
ed not in sighs and tears, but in the pomp of
the funeral and in the multitude of persons
assisting."‡

To add to the solemnity of a funeral service,
our ancestors in the faith employed torches,
incense, music, and the tolling of bells. I shall
speak of these more at length, when treating
on the resurrection of the body, as preached
by the cemetery. All these rites, so useful to
the dead, were for our forefathers, as they are
for ourselves, a source of much consolation to
the living. Hence their deep distress when

---

* Epist. I. ad Jacob. Frat. Dom.
† Contr. Cels. lib. vi. and viii.
‡ Epist. ad Paulam, De Obitu Blesillæ.

prohibited to chant at a funeral. "Who can recall to mind," says Victor, Bishop of Utica, " without shedding tears, the occasion when the tyrant compelled us to follow our dead to the grave in silence, without even the chanting of a hymn ?"* Long before the hour of interment, touching evidences of fraternal charity were made manifest: they began on the preceding evening. During the night, the office called the vigils, or watchings, was chanted not only in the churches, but also in the mortuary chamber itself. In memory of this old custom, the office is still sung on the eve of a funeral in the diocese of Besançon.

I will conclude with two remarkable examples. The body of the Emperor Constantine was carried to the tomb on a bier of state, covered with flowers, amid burning torches and the chanting of hymns. " Never," says Eusebius, " since the beginning of the world was witnessed such magnificence."†

The funeral of St. Germain, Bishop of Auxerre, was a grand triumphal march. This illustrious prelate, having died at Ravenna, his body was carried to Auxerre, a distance of six hundred miles, accompanied by a large

---

* De Persecut. Vandalor. lib. i.
† Euseb. in Vita Constan. lib. iv. c. lxiii.

concourse of persons. All along the route the greatest respect was evinced by the people, who came out to level the roads and build special bridges. The air resounded with the voices of the chanters, was redolent with incense, and at night, the darkness was dispelled by the light of countless torches.

At the ordinary funeral service, the priest, after having performed the " Libera," gives the signal for departure, by intoning the beautiful and consoling antiphon : " May the angels conduct thee to Paradise ; at thy coming may the angels meet thee, and lead thee into the heavenly city of Jerusalem." During the singing of these last words, and on the conclusion of the above ceremonies, all of which are so many undoubted evidences of respectful affection for the deceased, and a solemn acknowledgment of the undying fraternal charity between the living and dead, the cemetery, at last, admits the sacred deposit, confided to its care until the day of resurrection.

What a contrast between Catholic burial and the brutal proceedings of the " solidaires"! Let us congratulate ourselves on being children of the Church, while we pray for those who are not, or who, having been, are no longer such.

EIGHTEENTH LETTER.

MY DEAR FRIEND:

We have already listened to two sermons preached to us by the cemetery, on the *Sanctity of the human body, and on the Brotherhood of the children of God on both sides of the grave.* I have listened to many orators, but in my opinion, no one ever preached these fundamental truths with equal power. In the two following sermons, its eloquence will be no less impressive and plain. We are going to hear all about the immortality of the soul and the resurrection of the flesh. You will admit that in point of sublimity, importance, and practical utility, no better subject could be chosen.

" If you inquire," says the cemetery, " why I have been so solemnly consecrated and hedged in with so much reverence, I reply that I am a reliquary designed to receive something holy. This holy and thrice holy relic is your body. As I am sanctified by a body, the body is sanctified by the soul. The body has been a temple, a sanctuary, a reliquary occupied by the soul, which is the living image of the God of all sanctity." To the cemetery, therefore, the human body is not what it is to the " solidaire," a clod of mean earth. That the body is purified and sanctified by prayer and holy rite out of regard to the soul, is clear from the meaning of the prayers and ceremonies employed before it is carried to the grave. It is time for me to redeem my promise of explaining some of these. The corpse is laid upon the catafalque in the church. Around this catafalque, you see burning tapers, while the holy-water vase stands at the foot. The smoke of incense rises, as prayers are poured forth, and soon the hymn is intoned, awakening in our souls ineffable emotions of mingled joy and sadness. What does all this mean ?

St. Chrysostom replies : " What mean these torches whose brightness delights my eyes ?

They tell us that we are escorting our dead, as if they were athletes coming forth victorious from the combat. What mean these chants? In them we glorify God, and thank Him for having given the crown to him who has just left us, for having delivered him from all the ills of life, and for having placed him near Himself, beyond the reach of fear. Is not this good cause for our hymns and psalms? Are they not proofs of our happiness and joy? Why should there be tears and lamentations in the presence of immortality?"*

How absurd this illumination, how unmeaning these joyous canticles, if man had no soul; or if the soul did not survive the body; or if, as infidels pretend, the body had been and still were a mere clod of earth!

The prayers, incense, and holy-water have their meaning too. "It is certain," says St. Athanasius, "that if the dead were not benefited thereby, we should cease to honor them by mementoes in the holy sacrifice, and by the cares of sepulture. But our very eyes tell us the contrary. When the vine on the distant hill-side begins to blossom, the wine in your cellars is conscious of the blossoming, and

---

* Homil. iv. in Epist. ad Hebr. n. 5, opp. t. xii. pars prior, p. 66, edit. Gaume.

sensitive to its influence. Thus material things of earth give us an idea how the souls of sinners are affected favorably by the unbloody sacrifice."*   In these words, the great doctor interprets the universal faith.   You know that praying for the dead is as ancient as the world itself, and as widespread as is the human family. It is practiced even by pagan savages.   This you will soon see, as we develop one more proof of the indestructible faith of all nations in the existence and immortality of the soul.

Nothing could be more touchingly expressive than the Catholic funeral-prayers.   First, we hear the voice of the dead issuing from the coffin : " Deliver me, O Lord! from eternal death, on that dreadful day, when the heavens and the earth shall be moved, and Thou shalt come to judge the world by fire.   I tremble and am seized with the fear of judgment and of the wrath to come."†

The living respond, " Yes, when the heavens and the earth shall be moved."   This inimitable dialogue continues.   The deceased says, " That day of wrath and misery, that great day of calamity and bitterness."   The living respond, " When thou shalt come to judge

* De Variis Quæst. Quæst 34.
† Roman Ritual.

the world by fire." The voice of the dead is stilled, while all the living send up to the sovereign Judge this supplication for mercy: "Eternal rest give unto him, O Lord! and let perpetual light shine upon him." To help obtain this ineffable happiness, the priest uses incense and holy-water. Making the circuit of the catafalque, he sprinkles the coffin, and then incenses it. By the holy-water, so formidable to the devil, he drives away those evil spirits who so often practice their fury against the body of the departed, in order to injure in death what they could not harm in life. Incense, the emblem of prayer, recalls the good works of the dead person, and reminds us of the efficacy of the prayers of the living in behalf of the dead. Christians of every age have recognized in the mingling of incense and holy-water, another sign of the union between the living and the dead.

These highly instructive ceremonies and tender prayers compose the service of the " Libera," a word which means deliverance. severance of all the bonds which could chain down the soul of the deceased ; and freedom from all those powerful enemies which could prevent the body from resting in peace. The *Libera* concludes by a prayer in which the

priest reminds the Almighty that it is His pro-
vince to be merciful, to spare, and to pardon;
humbly conjuring Him to receive in His infinite mercy this soul whose exile is just over,
and to introduce it into the company of the
angels of heaven, there to enjoy eternal happiness forever.

Where can you find, my dear Frederic, a
plainer and more eloquent demonstration of
the Catholic faith in the existence and immortality of the soul? This faith is further evi-
denced by the alms contributed in behalf of
the deceased, by the crowns of immortelles
placed on the tomb, the evergreens planted in the ground, and also by the very position of the body in the grave. According
to Catholic custom, the face should be up-
ward, looking heavenward, the head to the
West and the feet to the East; meaning
that by occupying this position, the deceased professed his hopes, prays, and is
ready to leave the West and march toward
the East.

Finally, the cross standing at the head of
his grave, erect like the great mast of a ship
submerged beneath the sea, but not entirely
broken up, proclaims that death is not a complete shipwreck of man; that life dwells in

the tomb, guarded by God, who will bring it forth to light on the last day.

I can not bring this letter to a close in any more appropriate way than by exclaiming with you: What an admirable preacher the cemetery is!

NINETEENTH LETTER.

ALL THE PRAYERS FOR THE DEAD PROCLAIM THE IMMORTAL-
ITY OF THE SOUL.—PRAYERS ON THE THIRD, SEVENTH,
THIRTIETH, AND FORTIETH DAYS—ANNIVERSARY SERVICES
—THE DEAD AWARE OF OUR PRAYERS—CATHOLIC TEACH-
ING.

MY DEAR FRIEND:

As we have just seen, all the prayers for the dead proclaim belief in the immortality of the soul. Among Catholics, these prayers do not cease with the closing of the grave. They are renewed and repeated at stated periods, fixed by venerable tradition : indeed, they are continual. These periods are the third, seventh, thirtieth, and fortieth days after death, and the anniversary. What is the meaning of choosing these fixed days? The answer to this question will be the subject of the present letter. But first, a few words about the Office for the Dead, that ancient rite so replete with holy recollections, and dating its origin back to the Old Testament. When Jacob died,

180

Joseph and his brethren, accompanied by a great concourse of the Egyptians, brought his father's body to Hebron. Great mourning, however, had been held previously in Egypt for the space of forty days, which was repeated for the space of seven days at the threshing-floor of Atad, beyond the Jordan. This great and vehement mourning means not only weeping and lamenting, but the prayers and sacrifices offered in favor of the dead.

The same thing was done at the death of Moses, Aaron, and their sister Miriam. It would be wrong to suppose that these are isolated cases in the history of God's people. You know that these functions were continued from age to age, down to the time of the Machabees. Such is the biblical authorization of our Office for the Dead. Under the new law, we are indebted for this office, in its primitive form, to the Apostles themselves, and, in its more finished and perfect form, to Origen, one of the most venerable and learned fathers of the early Church. We find a peculiarity in this office which does not exist in any other. Although it has its first vespers, it has no second ; meaning by this, that the office can recognize but one period of time for man without hinting at the beginning of another ;

for the bodies of the saints being once delivered from pain, are delivered for all eternity.

Why, my dear Frederic, are we not better
acquainted with the meaning of most of the
institutions and practices of the Church?
Why do so many Christians live and die in
ignorance of the most of them? Where could
the clergy find a more prolific source of tender
and practical instructions, both for themselves
and the people, than in frequent explanation
of these ancient and highly instructive rites?
But why look for impossibilities? This deplorable ignorance is at once the necessary
and inevitable result of our pagan education,
and a practical proof of its pernicious effects,
even upon the clergy.

Let us now consider the days appointed by
the Church for the solemn repetition of the
Office for the Dead. The first in turn is the
" third day," chosen with a view of remind-
ing us of the three days passed by Our Lord
in the sepulchre, ending with the third
glorious day of His resurrection, a day full of
hope and consolation for us. The " seventh
day," uniting the Old and New Testament,
and replete with recollections of remotest
antiquity, gives rise to an act of religion that
dates from the beginning of time. Its obser-

vance supplies us with abundant instruction. We celebrate the office, then, on the seventh day, if not on each of the seven, after the example of the sons of Jacob, who mourned their father during seven days. Another reason for the recital of these "seventh day" prayers is to obtain for the deceased the remission of all the sins committed during his whole life, and symbolized by the length of time expended in the creation, that is, seven days, ending of course with the seventh day of rest.

The observance of the "thirtieth day" is equally venerable for its traditions, and equally important by reason of its aims and intentions. It is in accordance, then, with the spirit of our mother, the Church, that we celebrate mass for the dead during the thirty days immediately succeeding the day of death, and also on the thirtieth day itself. One reason for this observance is to perpetuate the remembrance of the thirty days' mourning over Jacob by his sons, and over Moses and Aaron by the Israelites. The second reason is, because three times ten are thirty. The number three signifies the Blessed Trinity, and the number ten the precepts of the decalogue. We pray, therefore, three times ten days for the dead, in order to obtain for them, through divine mercy, remission of all their sins against the Holy Trinity, and against the precepts of the decalogue.*

The "fortieth day" represents the forty hours that our Lord remained in the sepulchre previous to His resurrection. It also gives expression to the ardent desires of all the living faithful to see their departed brethren come forth one day gloriously from the tomb as did the First-born among the dead.

The "anniversary" is a day no less scrupulously observed, and no less sacred than the others just mentioned. Most Catholics observe it by having a special mass offered up, reciting various prayers, and giving alms. Like the others, it is founded in the affection entertained by the living for the dead, and is eminently useful to both.

Thus, one year after the death of our friends, we pray that their years of exile may be replaced by endless years of happiness in heaven. As we celebrate the annual festivals of the saints, both to honor them, and to rouse ourselves to an imitation of their virtues, so do we keep sacred the anniversaries of our dead in order to assist them, and to awaken our own devotion toward them. Finally, we offer

---

* Cornel. a Lapide.

these annual prayers, because, as St. Augustine says, " Not knowing with certainty the condition of our friends in the other world, we prefer to do too much for them rather than too little."

Is there any thing more commendable, my dear Frederic, than this observance of certain days, set apart ages ago, for the express purpose of bringing relief to the suffering souls in purgatory? As they come along at stated intervals on the journey of life, they seem as so many preachers who unite their voices with that of the cemetery, to proclaim the immortality of the soul. Even the pagans who lived before Christ had special prayers for their dead on the third, seventh, ninth, twentieth, thirtieth, and fortieth days after their death. Misguided by the arch-enemy of truth, these people built up a temple of superstition on an old foundation of truth. As soon as Christianity came into the world, she reclaimed her property and divested it of all heathen impurities.

It may be useful before closing this letter to elucidate a question connected naturally with our subject. It is this : Are the dead cognizant of our prayers? An affirmative answer to this question may be found in the article of faith which we pronounce every day, " I believe in the communion of saints." Although the faithful departed have left this earth, they have not ceased to live, nor have they ceased to be members of the Church. There are three dwelling-places for the large family of the Heavenly Father—the earth, purgatory, and heaven. The inhabitants are united by the golden chains of indissoluble brotherhood. This union, being founded on charity, becomes practical in the assistance that one branch affords to the other. The saints pray for us, and we pray for the souls in purgatory, who, in their turn, will repay us with interest for all that we do for them. This is an article of our faith.

But how can the souls in purgatory know any thing about our prayers? Catholic theology replies, " The departed souls have four ways of knowing what good works we do in their behalf. First, by direct revelation from God; secondly, through the ministry of angels; thirdly, through the reports brought to them by the countless souls arriving every minute in purgatory, from all parts of the globe; and fourthly, by the very perceptible decrease in their sufferings." * As we know

---

* St. Thomas, 1 p. q. 89, article 8.

that the lost souls in hell are ignorant of what is going on among the living, except as God may permit them, now and then, to catch a glimpse of earth ; so, too, the souls in purgatory, as they do not yet enjoy the beatific vision, know nothing about what is going on in the world, except through the means just mentioned. But the saints, being already in the enjoyment of God, know every thing that takes place here below. Such is the opinion of St. Gregory the Great, who asks, " What can be concealed from those who see God, who Himself sees all things ?" There are some persons, however, who maintain that the saints know nothing more than what is necessary to their happiness and ours.*

Our duty is, therefore, my dear Frederic, to love and preserve these sacred relations existing between ourselves and the dead ; for we may feel assured that in assisting them, we help ourselves, and further the wise designs of a merciful God.

---

* St. Thomas.

TWENTIETH LETTER.

DEAR FRIEND:

The existence and immortality of the soul, the communion of saints, the utility of praying for the dead, all so eloquently preached to us by the cemetery, are articles, not only of Christian faith, but they have always been believed among pagans.

Except a few sensual Epicureans of antiquity, worthy precursors of our modern " solidaires," all nations have believed in these fundamental truths. To find evidence, let us take a bird's-eye view of the world. We will wing our flight first to Palestine, the ancient home of the Jews, whom we will follow in their wanderings through all parts of the globe. The Old Testament teaches the immortality of the soul in countless places ; telling us over and over again that the souls of

188

the dead were gathered to their fathers; that is, that they outlived their bodies. Lest I should tire you by my tediousness, I will merely mark in a note at the bottom of this page the passages of Holy Scripture having a bearing on this truth, and showing the belief held by the Jewish people.*

The use of the term *scheol* is an indication of their faith in the life of the soul after its separation from the body; for it means the place where souls met each other. You know that the Pentateuch never employs this word in the sense of a tomb or grave. Thus in Genesis we read that, when Jacob heard of Joseph's death, he exclaimed, " I will go down to my son into hell (scheol) mourning." (Gen. 37 : 35.) It is evident that he did not mean the grave, for he thought that his son had been devoured by beasts. This doctrine, revealed by God to the fathers of the human family, was preserved by His providence from generation to generation. Thus, in addressing Moses, He calls Himself the God of Abraham, the God of Isaac, and the God of Jacob, long after their death. Now, God can not be God of

---

* Gen. 37 : 35; 25 : 28; 35 : 29; Numb. 60 : 26; Deut. 32 : 50; Jud. 11 : 10; IV. Kings 22 : 20; II. Paralip. 34 : 28; Wisdom, 3 : 1; Isai. 26 : 19; I. Mach. 14 : 30; II. Mach. 7 : 9; 14 : 23.

what does not exist. He is God only of that which is, and consequently lives. Hence those patriarchs, whose God He declared Himself to be, were not entirely dead. Their souls were living somewhere. And as He had been their God during their pilgrimage on earth, so He continued to be their God after they had escaped from exile, and entered their own true country. It was in this way that the Jews of Our Saviour's time understood these words of God. One person asks Him what to do to gain eternal life. Martha professes, in the hearing of Christ, that she knows her brother Lazarus will rise again at the last day, thus showing that she believed he was not annihilated, or dead, body and soul.

However, there was among the Jews, a sect called Sadducees, who having imbibed from the Greeks some of the doctrines of Epicurus, began to deny the immortality of the soul. You know with what success and power Our Lord shut their mouths and brought them to shame and confusion in the presence of the delighted multitude. " And Jesus answering, said to them, You err, not knowing the Scriptures, nor the power of God, . . . nor read that which was spoken by God, saying to you, I am the God of Abraham, and the God of Isaac, and the God of Jacob. He is not the God of the dead, but of the living." (Matt. 22 : 29–32.) This reply of the Divine Master is a complete refutation, or what is called an argument *ad hominem*, because it goes direct to the point, using the adversary's own weapons. Hence the plaudits of the bystanders. A word will make you understand this better. To refute' these Sadducees, Our Lord selected a passage from the Pentateuch : " I am the God of Abraham, the God of Isaac, and the God of Jacob." He passed over many equally conclusive arguments to be found elsewhere in Scripture, because the only portion admitted by the Sadducees was the Pentateuch ; these books were held in high esteem among the Jews, while the three patriarchs were so much revered that no person would dare to say that they were dead, that is, annihilated in body and soul. All believed that they dwelt with God and kept watch and care over their posterity.*

After their dispersion, the Jews carried with them, whithersoever they went, the doctrine of the soul's immortality. To-day, they call their burying-places *the homes of the living ;* and as they lay the bodies of their deceased

---

* Corn. a Lapide,

brethren in their graves, they thus address them: " Blessed be God who made you. He knows you, one and all, and will raise you up to life on the last day." Then each one throws on the coffin a handful of clay.*

We will now take a glance at heathendom. Ælianus relates that, " when Cercides of Megalopolis was asked on his death-bed, if he were willing to die, he replied, Why not? I am pleased to leave this body ; for then I shall ascend to that country where I shall meet Pythagoras among the philosophers, Homer among the poets, and Apollo among the musicians, together with others illustrious in the arts and sciences."† Xenophon gives us the last advice of Cyrus to his sons: " Do not suppose, my dear children, that when I shall have left this life, I shall be nothing or nowhere. You have never seen my soul, yet you believe that my body was its dwelling-place. Believe that my soul will be the same to you, even after it is parted from the body."‡ It is said that Cato killed himself, while reading Plato's book on the immortality of the soul, in order the sooner to enjoy that

* Cérémon. Funèb. Published by J. F. Bernard, 1818.
† Ælian. lib. xiii.
‡ Xenophon. Cyrop.

immortal life. Cicero puts the following words in Scipio's mouth long after his death: " Be assured that all those who have labored for the preservation, defense, and welfare of their country will enjoy eternal happiness in heaven. . . . Men live in reality only when they have broken the bonds of the flesh and come out of its prison. What you call your life is death."*

Leaving the Greeks and Romans, let us visit the Indians, and we shall find them all unchanged and unchangeable in their belief in the immortality of the soul. Among the laws of the Brahmins is the following: It is proper for the widow to be burned with her husband's corpse; and by so doing, accompany him to paradise, where they will dwell together for all eternity. The Peguans believe in transmigration of souls, which is nothing else than belief in the perpetual life of the soul, and a distorted view of the resurrection. In the island of Ceylon, the friends of the deceased call in their priests to recite prayers for the repose of the departed soul. We find the same manifestations of a belief in immortality among the islanders of Java and Sofala. The Sofalese are so firmly convinced that their de-

* De Repub. lib. vi.

ceased friends still live, that they prepare food
for them.

Winging our way to the great countries of
the East, we find the Chinese so devoted to
the souls of their dead ancestors that they
fall into idolatry. Should a "solidaire"
go there to tell them that their forefathers
were but clods of dirt, he would be burnt
alive. There is a law in Persia requiring
children to hold a funeral festival after their
parents' death, the object of which is to secure
rest and happiness to their relatives.

Penetrate into unhappy Africa, the most degraded portion of the globe, and there meet
the missionaries and travelers who will inter-
pret the religion of the inhabitants. Except-
ing a very few tribes, they all believe in the immortality of the soul. When the king of Da-
homey dies, hundreds of human beings are
put to death, that they may act as his guard of
honor in the next world. Only last year, on
the death of the late king, twenty-four women
were slain for the purpose of ministering to
him in the other life. In Congo, the rites at
a funeral are manifold, and most of them indicative of a firm belief that the dead man's
spirit still lives somewhere. Among nearly
all the other tribes may be found barbarous

and cruel practices ; but yet all demonstrating the same belief.

Throughout the American continent, we find that the aborigines believed in the immortality of the soul, and even in some sort of a resurrection. Not even the most degraded tribes could be charged with treating their dead as mere clods of earth. The early missionaries of Canada inform us that the tribes in those parts believed in the transmigration, and of course the immortality, of the soul. " They conduct their funerals," writes a traveler, " with all the pomp they can command. They paint the face of the corpse in various colors, lay it in a highly polished coffin, and surround it with palisades. The dead are sent to the other world well provided. New shoes, an axe, porcelain necklaces, a pipe, tobacco, cooking utensils, meat, and other articles of food, are placed near them. These are intended for the use of the deceased in that beautiful country, the ' happy hunting-grounds.' Such is their notion of heaven. They also have feasts in honor of the dead, on which occasion they take the bones from the old grave, decorate them with porcelain rings, and then bury them in another place. This ceremony they believe to be gratifying to the departed souls. In fact, all the American tribes carry out scrupulously their accustomed modes of honoring the dead."*

After their battles, the prisoners are distributed among the victors, especially among the women who have lost their husbands and brothers. If the women wish, they may put them to death, saying, " My father, my husband, or my brother," as the case may be, " has no slaves to wait upon him in the land of the dead ; you must, therefore, go to him without delay." The prisoners are then cruelly slain.† Believing in the immortality of the soul, they locate their heaven amid the stars, and their hell in the wild mountain recesses. In Central and South-America, similar practices were known to exist among the native Indians, being undoubted expressions of faith in the undying nature of the soul. In his work on Peru, Lopez de Gomara tells us, that when the Spaniards opened the tombs of the Peruvian chiefs, the Indians besought them not to disturb the bones, lest they would not be all together in one place at the time of the resurrection ; thus showing their faith in the immortality of the soul and

---

* Cérémon. Funèb. t. i. p. 35. † Ibid. p. 37.

the resurrection of the body. It was because of this belief, that the wives and servants of the dead volunteered to die, that they might serve them in the other world.

In the islands of Otaheite, when a native approaches a burial-place, he uncovers his body down to the waist, and assumes an attitude of respect. Their funerals are attended with lamentation and prayer.

We might extend our travels, but I will end them by relating an event, for the account of which we are indebted to Captain Wilson, an English navigator. His ship was lying at anchor in the Southern Ocean off the Pelew Islands. It was Sunday, and the crew had assembled on deck for divine service. The king's son was present, and after prayers the captain began to explain the service, saying, " We pray that we may become better men. For when we die and are buried, we will then live again in heaven." The prince replied, " We do the same thing in Pelew. Wicked men remain in the earth, good men go to heaven and become beautiful."

All these savage and pagan nations are so many prodigal sons, who have squandered the greatest part of the inheritance of truth given to them by the Great Father of the human family.   To the disgrace of the " solidaires," they have preserved the knowledge of the soul's immortality.

TWENTY-FIRST LETTER.

My Dear Frederic:

The sanctity of the human body, the indivisible brotherhood of man on both sides of the grave, and the immortality of the soul, have thus far been the subjects of the sermons preached to us by the voice of the cemetery. The whole world has been listening to its voice from time immemorial, and its warnings have been widely heeded. For the truths delivered have been so deeply graven in the soul of man as to become a part of his nature; and neither the gross vices of barbarism, the refined indulgence of the passions, nor the false reasoning of learned impiety could tear them out.

Our eloquent preacher has in reserve one more subject—the resurrection of the body; a subject full of consolation, and forming the complement of the other three.

How does the cemetery treat this new subject? Let it answer for itself: " I preach the resurrection of the flesh, by my very name, cemetery signifying a dormitory or place for sleeping.* The dormitory supposes sleep, and sleep implies an awakening. I am not a land that devours its inhabitants; I am a reliquary to preserve them. All who repose on my bosom are not dead but sleeping. Your father and mother, your lamented brother and beloved sister lie here; but they are asleep. ' The girl is not dead, but sleepeth.' "

The word cemetery is scarce born into existence when the golden-mouthed Chrysostom rises to explain it: " How beautifully and aptly the name suits the object! How full of consolation and wisdom! It is really true, then, that death is no longer death, but a sleep, or a sweet slumber. We are assembled here to-day, (Good-Friday,) in commemoration of Our Lord's descent among the dead, and the place where we are assembled is termed a cemetery, that you may understand they are

---

* The Greek word Κοιμητήριον means dormitory.

not dead who lie here, but sleeping. Before
the coming of Christ, death was truly named
death.   But since He came, and brought life
into the world by suffering death, death has
become a sleep, a gentle slumber.   He Himself named it thus, and His disciples imitated
Him.   'Lazarus   our   friend,'   said   Jesus,
'sleepeth.'   (John 11 : 11.)   He does not say
Lazarus is dead, although he really was so.
It is plain that this term was an unusual
name for death; for the Apostles were puz-
zled, nay, even took the expression in its lite-
ral sense, saying, 'Lord, if he sleep, he shall
do well.' (John 11 : 12.)"

St. Paul, in several of his epistles, calls
death a sleep, and speaks of the dead as fallen
asleep in the Lord.   Nowhere is he more explicit than in his first epistle to the Thessa-
lonians: " And we will not have you ignorant, brethren, concerning them that are
asleep, that you be not sorrowful, even as
others who have no hope.   For if we believe
that Jesus died and rose again, even so them
who have slept through Jesus, will God bring
with Him." (1. Thess. 4 : 12, 13.)

" See," continues St. Chrysostom, " how
death is everywhere termed sleep. For this
reason the place where the dead repose is

called a cemetery, which word means a place for sleeping, a dormitory, and is full of hope and comfort. Therefore, when you bring hither a dead friend, be not disconsolate; for you are not consigning him to death, but to sleep. Remember the name of the place to which you are bringing him—dormitory; death's bonds having been burst asunder by the death of Christ."

Who burst these bonds asunder and broke down the prison of death, to earn for the cemetery its appropriate name? The eloquent patriarch will tell us. Listen attentively, my dear Frederic, to language which pagan elegance could never equal.

"'To-day, Our Lord visited hell. On this day He shattered its brazen gates; on this day He broke its iron bolts.'* How correct these expressions are! He does not say, He *opened* the brazen gates, but He *shattered* them; thus rendering the prison unavailing forever. Instead of drawing the bolts, He broke them, rendering further imprisonment impossible. When the Son of God pulls down, who will dare to build up?

Up to the time of the Messiah, no one had been able to compel death to relinquish a

---

* Isa. 45 2.

single captive ; but when He appeared in the dark prison of the dread enemy, His omnipotence set them all free."

How do you designate the victory by which the Divine Conqueror acquired a right to claim these prisoners of death? Hear St. Chrysostom once more: " The Saviour first chained the 'strong man armed,' and then despoiled him of those treasures, called by the prophet Isaiah the dark invisible treasures. And in truth they were enveloped in darkness until the Sun of Justice, arising over them, *converted their hell into a heaven.*"

The prophet Isaiah had good reason for calling death a treasury of darkness, for it held very many valuable treasures. "All humanity, that real treasure belonging to God, but stolen by the devil when Adam fell, was imprisoned under the empire of death. Like to a good and wise ruler, who, in his efforts to benefit his subjects, captures some arch-thief, who, at the head of his hordes, has been plundering the country and hiding his booty in a dark cavern ; whom he chains as prisoner, hands him over to justice, and removes his spoils to the safe-keeping of lawful authority. This is what Christ has done. After having put death in chains, He carries off His treasures, namely, the human race. St. Paul teaches this truth in the following words: ' He hath delivered us from the power of darkness, and hath transported us into the kingdom of the Son of His love.'"*

How much, then, my dear Frederic, is expressed by the word cemetery! The "solidaires" themselves can not pronounce the word without condemning themselves and their theories in the very act, and professing unconsciously the most consoling article in the creed of civilized nations.

The cemetery has two other names in Catholic language, both indicative of resurrection; namely, Holy Field, and Field of God. In Italy, it is usually called *Campo Santo*, holy field, and properly so. You know that the Republic of Pisa, one of the greatest maritime powers of the middle ages, sent out a fleet to the Holy Land for the purpose of bringing home cargoes of the soil of Judea, which had been consecrated by the footprints of Jesus. With this soil, they made their cemetery of *Campo Santo*.

Why this vast expense? Ask the faithful of these heroic ages, and they will reply, " There is nothing more noble or more sacred

---

* Coloss. 1 : 13.

in our estimation than a human body destined to a glorious immortality; and no earth is more worthy of forming its resting-place while awaiting judgment than the earth moistened by the tears and consecrated by the footprints of our Saviour. These are the reasons why we have spared no expense or trouble in preparing our bed, which is also to be the bed of our children and fellow-citizens." The Pisans, however, had been anticipated in a similar profession of faith. You remember how the Empress Helena, during her pious pilgrimage to Palestine, had the field of blood, Haceldama, dug up, and the soil brought in royal galleys even to Rome. This field had been bought by the Jews, and paid for with the treason-money of Judas, in order to furnish free burial to strangers. To carry out this design to the letter, none but pilgrims and strangers are allowed to be buried in this soil. You remember this venerable burying-place near the Vatican.

The other appellation, Field of God, is a very expressive one. God, the Creator, restorer, and preserver of all things, is like the husbandman sowing his seed. Every husbandman has his field. God has His in the cemetery and near His house, the church.

Whilst the farmer sows various kinds of seed, God sows but one kind in His field. The farmer plants his with full confidence of soon seeing it rise above the surface, to reward his pains in due time, by ample returns. He is not disappointed.

The seed sown by God in His field is the most choice, the most precious, the most highly prized of all seeds ; for it is a human body formed to its Maker's likeness, redeemed by a Saviour's blood, the heir to eternal happiness and joy. We have seen with what jealous care, God watches over this seed and the field where it is sown. Time is the season of sowing; eternity will be the harvest-season when the whole human race will be ripe for its future rewards or punishments.

It is then, that man's body, after having undergone in the earth a process similar to that gone through by the grain of wheat, will appear to our eyes glorious, luminous, agile, subtile, and impassible. As the grain of wheat owes its new modification to the undying principle of life implanted in it, namely, the creative word of God, so will our body owe its glorious resurrection and its eternal happiness to the divine germ planted within us by the Redeemer, at our union with Him in Holy Communion *in re* or *in voto.*

But let us remember, my dear friend, that we must first die, before we can have a resurrection. Let us die then to the old man of sin, that we may rise new men. As the seed in the ground throws off all that has not the principle of life, let us cast off all that is not of God, and for God. This is an indispensable condition of a glorious immortality; it is the law of our union with the new Adam. " For if we have been planted together in the likeness of His death, we shall be also in the likeness of His resurrection "*

While we are awaiting this much-desired day, let us throw off sin, die to ourselves, pass through the world as the bird does through the air, without stopping for wind or rain. *Sic transeamus per bona temporalia, ut non amittamus æterna.* Let us so pass through temporal things that we may not lose the eternal.

---

* Rom. 6 : 5.

TWENTY-SECOND LETTER.

THE CEMETERY A PLACE OF TEMPORARY REST—OUR LORD'S TEACHINGS—HE FORETELLS HIS OWN RESURRECTION—DEATH IS BUT SLEEP—CITATION FROM ST. PAUL—FROM ST. JOHN—PAGAN OPPOSITION—THE FATHERS OF THE CHURCH.

MY DEAR FREDERIC:

When we say that the cemetery is a place of rest for those who fall asleep in the Lord, we but state the common belief of all men in the resurrection; that is, in the future restoration to life of all generations of every age, clime, and religion. We have heard and seen this truth proved. Although the belief in a future resurrection was very much obscured by passion and ignorance, yet it was restored to its primitive purity by the Divine Preceptor of men. Listen to His teachings, and those of His apostles, on this point, and you will easily recognize the echo of their doctrines, in the very word *dormitory*, as applied to the cemetery.

Our Saviour was in Jerusalem. It was just

the hour for a repetition of the well-known miracle at the pond called Probatica. Great throngs of people were in attendance; some for the purpose of aiding their sick friends, but the majority had been brought by a desire to witness the performance of the miracle. And there was a certain paralytic there, unable to move from his bed, but patiently hoping that some kind hand would assist him into the water, when agitated by the angel. Our blessed Lord seeing him, advances to his bedside, and asks, " How long have you been paralyzed?" " For eight and thirty years," is the sad response of the helpless invalid. Jesus said, " Wilt thou be made whole?" "Alas! Sir, there is no one to carry me into the pond at the favorable moment." Moved to compassion, Our Saviour says to him, "Arise, take up thy bed, and walk." Imagine, if you can, the excitement that this miracle must have made among the thousands of spectators of every age, rank, and religion, there present.

Observe the admirable wisdom of the Divine Master. Why did He effect this instantaneous cure in Jerusalem, and in presence of so many eye-witnesses? To prepare their minds to receive the doctrine He was about to preach. and to confirm their belief in a far greater miracle than the healing of a poor paralytic; namely, the resurrection of all men on the last day.

Taking advantage of the astonishment of the Jews, Our Lord hastens to say, "For as the Father raiseth up the dead, and giveth life, so the Son also giveth life to whom He will. . . . Amen, amen, I say unto you, that the hour cometh, and now is, when the dead shall hear the voice of the Son of God, and they that hear shall live. For as the Father hath life in Himself, so He hath given to the Son also to have life in Himself. . . . Wonder not at this; for the hour cometh wherein all that are in their graves shall hear the voice of the Son of God. And they that have done good things, shall come forth unto the resurrection of life; but they that have done evil, unto the resurrection of judgment."*

It would be easy to multiply passages in which Our Lord asserts the doctrine of the resurrection. Sometimes He foretells His own resurrection in proof of His Divinity. Again, He terms death a sleep; as in the case of Lazarus, and that of the daughter of Jairus. On another occasion He speaks of the general

---

* John 5 : 21-29, *passim*.

judgment, when all men will appear before Him to be dealt with according to their works.

As I am writing a letter and not a treatise, I pass quickly from the Master to the disciples.

Hear St. Paul. After having shown that the belief in a resurrection of the body is the foundation of Christianity, and the keystone of human society, the great apostle continues, " But now Christ is risen from the dead, the first fruit of them that sleep. For by a man came death, and by a man the resurrection of the dead. And as in Adam all die, so also in Christ all shall be made alive."* St. Paul here alludes to a very profound but very evident truth, namely, that there are really but two men in history, the first Adam and the Second Adam. The first Adam is the origin of death ; the Second Adam is the principle of life. It is our union, or rather our identity, with the first Adam which has inflicted death upon us ; while union and identity with the Second Adam will restore us to life—the true life of which He is the principle. We may see, therefore, how indispensable is our union with Christ.

Dwelling upon this fundamental truth, St. Paul shows the stern necessity of the union

* I. Cor. 15 : 20-22.

that he has been speaking of. Then making use of the parable of the seed sown in the soil, he describes the glorious transformation operated in us by the resurrection. " But some man will say, How do the dead rise again, or with what manner of body shall they come? Senseless man, that which thou sowest is not quickened, except it die first. And that which thou sowest, thou sowest not the body that shall be, but bare grain, as of wheat, or of some of the rest. But God giveth it a body as He will, and to every seed its proper body. All flesh is not the same flesh ; but one is the flesh of men, another of beasts, another of birds, another of fishes. And there are bodies celestial, and bodies terrestrial : but one is the glory of the celestial, and another of the terrestrial. One is the glory of the sun, another the glory of the moon, and another the glory of the stars. For star differeth from star in glory.

" So also is the resurrection of the dead. It is sown in corruption, it shall rise in incorruption. It is sown in dishonor, it shall rise in glory ; it is sown in weakness, it shall rise in power. It is sown a natural body, it shall rise a spiritual body. If there be a natural body, there is also a spiritual body ; as it is

written, The first man Adam was made into
a living soul; the last Adam into a quicken-
ing spirit. Yet that was not first which was
spiritual, but that which is natural; afterward
that which is spiritual. The first man was
of the earth, earthly; the Second Man from
heaven, heavenly. Therefore, as we have
borne the image of the earthly, let us bear
also the image of the heavenly.

" Behold, I tell you a great mystery; we
shall all indeed rise again; but we shall not all
be changed."*

It is a necessary condition of our glorious
resurrection, that we so unite with the Second
Adam as to become His image, His disciples,
His children.

These words of St. Paul are so plain and
explicit that they render it unnecessary to
cite his other passages inculcating the same
doctrine. The mode of our resurrection we
shall see later.

The Apostle St. John is another preacher
of the resurrection. In his prophecies concerning the future condition of the Church,
both in time and eternity, he explains all her
mysteries most luminously—thanks to his
honored privilege of drawing his inspirations

---

* I. Cor. 15, *passim.*

from the very heart of his well-beloved Master, Our Lord Jesus Christ. " And I saw," he says, " a great white throne, and one sitting upon it, from whose face the earth and heaven fled away, and there was no place found for them. And I saw the dead, great and small, standing in the presence of the throne : and the books were opened ; and another Book was opened, which is the book of life ; and the dead were judged by those things which were written in the books according to their works : and the sea gave up the dead that were in it, and death and hell gave up their dead that were in them, and they were judged every one according to their works."*

This gathering of the dead, great and small, before the tribunal of the Sovereign Judge, proves not merely the immortality of the soul, but also the resurrection of the flesh ; and consequently the correctness of the term *dormitory* as applied to the cemetery. You will have an elucidation of this incontestable truth in my next letters.

We may thank the Gospel, that good messenger of truth and peace, for rescuing the comforting doctrine of the resurrection from the oblivion to which the Epicureans of anti-

---

* Apoc. 20 : 11–13.

quity would fain consign it. Peter preached it in Jerusalem; Paul before the philosophers of the Areopagus at Athens; Matthew to the Indians; Luke to the Gauls; and the other apostles to all nations. So the sun rose and shed its rays throughout the earth.

Paganism, however, did not yield without a struggle. When men with sinful and perverse hearts were told that they would have to answer for their evil doings, before an incorruptible judge, they took the alarm, and, with the fury of the tiger, rushed upon the apostles, who thus sealed with their blood the ancient faith of the human race.

Persecution by the tongue succeeded persecution by the sword. The devil, who knows so well how to raise fogs and gather clouds, aroused his agents and armed them against the truth of the resurrection with his own malice and hypocrisy. But Providence never fails. From the treasury of His infinite wisdom He brought forth lights—the brightest that ever shone among men, both in eloquence, depth of knowledge, and power of reasoning. Faithful to their inheritance, the religion of the Son of God and His apostles, they defended the mystery of the resurrection so successfully that they closed forever the mouths of their adversaries ; and the cemetery was again proved to be the place of rest for those who have fallen asleep in the Lord.

In the estimation of the sophists of old, the lessons of the Gospel were, as they are to-day to the "solidaires," nothing but assertions without proof. In their willful blindness, they would not see the miracles. The fathers of the Church, setting up their defense where the attack was most violent, proved by sensible evidences, by unanswerable arguments, the truth of divine teaching on a dogma at once comforting and frightful, namely, a future resurrection.

I will reserve their sayings for another letter.

TWENTY-THIRD LETTER.

My Dear Friend:

Let us read together, as an introduction to
the remaining letters, these luminous verses of
the Gospel: " Every one, therefore, that heareth these my words, and doth them, shall be
likened to a wise man, that built his house
upon a rock.   And the rain fell, and the floods
came, and the winds blew, and they beat upon
that house: and it fell not, for it was founded
on a rock.   And every one that heareth these
my words, and doth them not, shall be like
a foolish man that built his house upon the
sand.   And the rain fell, and the floods came,
and the winds blew, and they beat upon that
house : and it fell, and great was the fall
thereof."*

---

* Matt. 7 : 24-27.

If any man builds upon the sand, it is most certainly the victim of rationalism. The rationalistic philosopher is the man who, tearing himself from the saving guardianship of faith, pretends to discover the truth in his own small brain. As was the case in all ages, and is the case to-day, the edifice that he would build must rest on the shifting sands of human opinion. Time, experience, their own inherent contradictions, soon destroy these systems, leaving society strewn with the wrecks.

True philosophy is a very different thing. The genuine philosopher is that one who, standing upon the solid rock of faith, and taking Christian principles as his point of departure, explains to himself revealed dogmas, shows their dependence, their harmonies, and their conformity with reason; draws his consequences, and finally establishes those mighty propositions which subdue mind and heart by their truth and beauty. False philosophy and human passions combined will be powerless to undermine his edifice of truth; for being founded on a rock, it will last forever.

Such, my dear friend, is the grand and immortal philosophy of the fathers of the Church. You know that when our ancestors were marching on their expedition to the Holy Land, in order to effect the deliverance of the Saviour's sepulchre from the hands of the infidels, their oft-repeated war-cry was, *God wills it.* Thus, too, did the learned men of primitive Christianity come forward to deliver the doctrine of the resurrection from the hands of the false teachers, with the cry, " God wills it." He who once created man can again raise him from death to life. He *can*, and He *will*. This is our proposition.

He can. " And why," asks Tertullian, "could he not? Go back in thought to the moment of creation, and your incredulity will vanish. How was this world produced? Whence came the countless animals that were to inhabit the earth? Whence did the plants and trees, that at once covered the earth with beauty, derive the sap that circulated through all their parts? And yourself, O man! what were you before you were man? Nothing.

" If God, then, has brought you into existence out of nothing, why can He not raise you from death? You were not, and now you are. You will cease to live, and you will live again. Explain to me the mystery of your creation, and I will explain to you the mystery of your resurrection. Is it more difficult to be restored to what you once were, than to become what you once were not? It is certainly a greater work to produce than to repair, to create being than to merely modify it, to make a source of light than to kindle an extinguished torch. You have some materials to rebuild a fallen castle. God was pleased to precede the work of resurrection by the more wonderful and difficult one of creation."*

But you object, that this flesh of ours may be wasted in the waves, scattered by the winds, devoured by beasts, or even by men.

The potter who has made the vessel can mend it if it get broken; and you will not allow the Omnipotent to repair the work of His hands! Thanks to the very advanced state of science, the chemist can now dissolve the invisible ties uniting the elements of bodies, carry the analysis and decomposition of their parts to the infinite, so to speak; and then by a new process find these scattered atoms, separate them from thousands of others, bring them back, reunite them, and form new substances. Is it, then, impossible for God, who holds the universe in the hollow of His

---

* Tertullian, De Resurrectione Carnis, c. iii.

hand, to recover the scattered atoms of our bodies, reunite them, and restore them to their original condition ?

Tertullian continues, "Whether our flesh shall have lain at the bottom of the sea, been consumed by fire, devoured by wild beasts, or inclosed in the bosom of the earth whence it came, it is still within reach of God's mighty arm. He keeps it safely deposited against the day of a general resurrection, when He will unite it to the soul which formerly dwelt within it."* The words of the Apostle Paul, my dear friend, are very true, " Whether we live or whether we die, we are the Lord's." He watches over us, preserving in our flesh the vital principle planted there by Himself, just as He keeps it alive in the apparently dead grain of wheat buried in the field.

But, you add, our body is constantly changing, constantly throwing off and renewing its tissues. How can it ever be exactly as it was when inhabited by the soul? It matters but little that the body loses successively a certain number of its parts. For a body to be restored to life, it is not at all requisite that it recover all the particles of matter belonging

---

* Tertullian, ibid.   † Rom. 14 : 8.

to it at different periods of its existence. It is sufficient if the first elements, which form the groundwork or necessary essence of the human body, do not change while acquiring or losing these particles of accessory matter. And such is the case. You know this to be an indisputable fact, admitted by the most skillful observers, and plain even to the vulgar eye. The human countenance does not alter essentially, nor indeed any part of the body. Society treats the man at every stage of his living existence as the same person, and calls him always by the same name. Even the cannibal, at his dreadful banquets, does not acquire any thing essential and which he can not part with without continuing to be the same individual. Intelligent minds find no more difficulty in the question of the resurrection of his victims, than in that of men whose remains have been carefully deposited beneath the protecting marble.

Moreover, even the accidental particles of the human body do not go out of existence. Since the sixth day of creation, not an atom more or less of matter has existed in the universe. There has been modification, but no destruction. " The works which God hath made continue forever," saith the prophet.

*Omnia opera quæ fecit Deus, perseverant in perpetuum.** We defy the most skillful and persistent chemist, even with the most perfect instrument, to annihilate a grain of sand or a drop of water. To reduce being to nothing, is no less difficult than to produce being from nothing.

You see, my dear friend, that no reason can be given to show that our future resurrection exceeds the power of God, while the reason of all men affirms the possibility and even the certainty of this happy event.

Every body would laugh at the folly of a man who, imagining himself greater than any one else, would go out alone to challenge an immense army, and foolishly hope to win the victory. And yet the unbeliever, in the pride of his small and fallible intellect, makes himself equally ridiculous by setting up his individual judgment against the reasoning of all men, and his thoughts of an hour against the teachings of centuries.

But we shall rise again, for God is omnipotent. In our next we shall see that God wills it.

---

* Eccles. 3 : 14.

TWENTY-FOURTH LETTER.

WE SHALL RISE FROM THE DEAD—GOD'S ATTRIBUTES REQUIRE
IT—GOD'S TWO GREAT BOOKS—BOTH TEACH THE RESUR-
RECTION—THE UNIVERSE PREACHES THE RESURRECTION—
ST. CHRYSOSTOM—TERTULLIAN — ST. AUGUSTINE—TESTI-
MONY OF JOB AND ST. PAUL.

MY DEAR FRIEND:

We have seen that God *can* raise us from
the dead ; we shall now see that He *will* raise
us from the dead. His divine truth wills it,
His wisdom wills it, His justice wills it, His
goodness wills it.

His truth wills it. God has written two
great books, Nature, and the Bible. Both
proclaim the absolute and unchangeable will
of God to raise the human race from death to
life ; that is, to awaken from their sleep in the
vast dormitories, called cemeteries, all generations of men and women who have fallen
asleep in the Lord, since the beginning of
time.

Nature, as it preceded the Bible, is our
first book. " You ask me," says St. Chrysos-

tom, " how did God, before the invention of books, teach man to know him? By the same means that I have adopted to lead you to a knowledge of this Supreme Being. I have conducted you in spirit over all the universe, showing you the heavens, the earth, the ocean, the fields, and all the grand and varied riches of nature. We have descended to the very elementary origin of produced effects, and as we contemplated the magnificent prospect spread out before our minds, with united voices we cried out in transports of admiration, ' How great are Thy works, O Lord, how unfathomable thy ways !' "*

We shall presently discover in this grand volume of nature, not only the power, wisdom, and goodness of God, but also the effect of these divine attributes, namely, the mystery of the future resurrection.

" You inquire further," continues the illustrious patriarch, " why a book so useful as the Bible was not given by God to man from the beginning? Because God chose to teach man by objects or created beings, and not by books. Had he begun to teach us by certain characters, the learned only could take advantage of such means, which would be unavailing to the

---

* St. Chrys. Homil. 1. in Genes.

unlettered. The rich might procure this method of instruction, while the poor could not. To properly understand books, one should know the language in which they were first written. And so, the Bible, if it had been published in Greek or Latin, would have been useless to the Scythian, the Indian, the Egyptian, and to all strangers to those languages.

" This is not the case with the book of nature. Its language is intelligible to all men. It is accessible to the learned and the simple, to rich and poor. The psalmist does not say, The heavens witness the glory of God, but they *declare* it. The whole human race has heard this declaration, and seen its proof on the pages of the glorious spectacle around about them."

But how does the book of nature teach a coming resurrection? I see the question upon your lips, my dear Frederic, and I hasten to answer it. From what we have just heard, and from the still more explicit testimony of St. Paul, we learn that God created the world to manifest His glory, by setting it before our eyes as a mirror in which we may easily and plainly see the reflection of those spiritual realities that are invisible to our eyes. " For the invisible things of Him. . .

are clearly seen, being understood by the things that are made."* If you keep this principle in mind, you will easily understand how the fathers of the Church looked upon the book of nature as an untiring preacher of the resurrection.

First hear Tertullian : " The world presents to our view glorious evidence of God's power, and striking pictures of the resurrection. The expiring day sinks into the tomb of night. Darkness like a heavy pall hides from our sight the life and beauty of the earth. All nature is in silent mourning for its departed light. But soon the light breaks forth from its brief entombment, with all its former life and strength, the same as before. The sun has conquered its death of darkness, and torn away its winding-sheet of gloomy stillness. It is risen.

" The seasons are very suggestive of man's resurrection. At the approach of winter, trees, plants—all nature seems to die, but only to rise again to life and beauty in the spring. The grain is buried in the soil, there to be transformed and prepared for future utility and beauty.

" Our own existence is an unbroken succes-

* Rom. 1 : 20.

sion of deaths and resurrections. Is not a
sleeping man a picture of death ? And when
he awakes from sleep, does he not prefigure
his own awakening from the sleep of death,
on the morning of the great day ? In a word,
every thing in nature dies, and rises again to
life. This unceasing change in created things,
passing from life to death, and from death to
life, is palpable evidence of the future restoration of the human family. God stamped a
proof of this doctrine on every created thing,
long before it appeared in books. He taught
it by the effects of His power, before He
proclaimed it in Holy Scripture. He or-
dained Nature to be our first book, in order
to prepare our minds for the written word of
revelation. If we learn the first lesson, the
second will be easily mastered. We shall reason from what we see in nature, to that which
we are not permitted to see in revelation, save
by the eye of faith. When we behold ourselves constantly renewed, we shall easily believe that God will renew us after death for a
better life. If all creatures are again and
again renewed, for the sake and benefit of
man, how could it be that man himself would
not be restored for God, for whom he was
created ?"

Such are the lessons which these great men, with open eyes, clear minds, and pure souls, have learned from this great book of nature. Only the "solidaires," both ancient and modern, have failed to spell the first syllable in this plain and easy book of study. As St. Paul says, like the ass, the ox, and the mule, they can not see below the surface. " What things soever they naturally know, like dumb beasts, in these they are corrupted."*

As if to confirm the sayings of Tertullian, and to further prove that the greatest intellects have seen the mystery of the resurrection reflected in the mirror of nature, St. Augustin declares, " The whole economy of this world is a picture of the resurrection of the flesh. We see the trees drop their fruit, and lose their leaves and flowers at the approach of winter, only to regain them all in greater beauty and perfection when spring returns. I would ask the incredulous man, who doubts his future resurrection, where are now all these things that will greet your eyes at the proper season? Tell me where they are hidden. You can not find them; but God, who in His might brought them out of nothing, will, by His mysterious power, renew them again.

---

* Jude 10.

So will He renew our bodies on the last day.

"Observe the fields and meadows. When summer is over, they lose their flowers and grass. But in spring-time, the farmer's heart is gladdened at the sight of returning life and beauty. As the grass which died comes forth once more to life, so will our bodies come forth from the dust." *

You perceive, that in St. Augustine's opinion, the mystery of the resurrection is more frequently and more plainly written in the book of nature than any other dogma of our faith. *Tota hujus mundi administratio testimonium est resurrectionis futuræ.* All the fathers and doctors of the Church hold the same opinion.

It would be an unnecessary labor to cite any more of them ; so I will pass to the second book, in which God has foretold the mystery of the resurrection. Here, too, in order not to be tedious, I will confine myself to two pages of holy Scriptures—one from the Old Testament, another from the New.

It is now more than three thousand years since the world, and the pagan world, listened to Job's sublime profession of his faith in this

* St. Augustin. De Verbis Apostoli. Ser. 34.

mystery. He was the friend of God, and in-
herited and faithfully preserved the primitive
traditions. A great king among the princes
of the east, he fell, through the machinations
of the devil, from the summit of prosperity to
the lowest depths of wretchedness. Although
cast upon a dunghill, with his flesh rotting
from his bones, with every limb deformed,
and dying a living death, he never lost his
faith. Although, he exclaims, my spirit
shall be wasted, my days shall be shortened,
and the grave remaineth for me, my confidence is not shaken. " For I know that my
Redeemer liveth, and in the last day, I shall
rise out of the earth; and I shall be clothed
again with my skin, and in my flesh I shall
see my God. Whom I myself shall see, and
my eyes shall behold, and not another; this
my hope is laid up in my bosom."* We
thank Thee, O God! for having inspired this
profession of faith so many centuries ago.

Equally plain and explicit is the testimony
of St. Paul. " We shall all indeed rise again,
but we shall not all be changed. In a
moment, in the twinkling of an eye."† These
words need no comment, so I pass on.

You see, my dear friend, that the two great

---

* Job 19 : 25-27. † 1. Cor. 15 : 51 52.

books written by the hand of God for our instruction, the book of nature and the book of revelation, declare in the clearest language God's will to raise us from the dead. God must accomplish this mystery, or contradict Himself. He *can* do it; He *will* do it. And this is our hope laid up in our bosom. "*Reposita est hæc spes mea in sinu meo.*"-

TWENTY-FIFTH LETTER.

WE SHALL RISE AGAIN—GOD'S WISDOM DEMANDS IT—EVIDENCE—ALL NATIONS HAVE HELD THIS BELIEF—PRACTICE AMONG THE ROMANS—ARGUMENT OF TERTULLIAN—DIVINE JUSTICE REQUIRES OUR RESURRECTION TO LIFE.

MY DEAR FRIEND:

Divine wisdom requires that we should rise again after death. The wisdom of God is infallible in its reckonings, mild but firm in the means it uses to attain its end. What is the aim of divine wisdom in its relation to man? To make him happy, giving him life by the creative act, and restoring it to him again by redemption after he had lost it by disobedience. In this twofold favor which embraces within itself all other benefits, we must admire the master-stroke of Eternal Wisdom. On this two-fold act of goodness is based the whole history of the human race.

A man brought death into the world, and a man restored us again to life. Adam was a source of death, but Jesus Christ is the source of life. Our Saviour annihilated the principle of death in Adam, and having become the victor, burst forth from the sepulchre and took His rightful place in heaven. In the incarnation, our nature was united to His nature; He became our head, and we became His members, flesh of His flesh, and bone of His bone. His object was, to give us a share in Himself, in His life, in His glory, in His everlasting happiness. This object can be reached only through the resurrection.

Without this resurrection, God's wisdom would be defective, the world would be a monstrosity, and Christ would have died in vain. His death would have failed to restore us to our primitive rights. Christ, the Head, would be full of immortal life and resplendent in glory, while the other portions of His mystic body would rot in the darkness of eternal death. All humanity shrinks from such doctrine, and protests against a materialism that would degrade it to the level of the brute.

There is incontestable proof, that all nations held some sort of a belief in the resurrection. " The transmigration of souls, a doctrine taught by the most celebrated schools of philosophy, was nothing else," says Tertullian, "but a distorted view of the mystery of the resurrection."* What other explanation can you give to the prayers, funeral-rites, and offerings in favor of the dead, that we have seen practiced by all peoples, if they had no hope of a resurrection?

To mention one example. The Romans held two annual festivals in honor of the dead, called the FERALIA and the LEMURIA. At the former, which were held toward the end of February, offerings of fruits, flowers, bread, and wine were placed on the tomb-stones to appease the manes of the dead, while food was also prepared for them to partake of. The LEMURIA were held in May. The faithful observer of ancient rites arose at midnight, washed his hands three times, put nine black beans into his mouth, and afterward threw them behind his back, saying, "With these beans I ransom myself and my dead." Could there be any more striking proof of a pagan's belief in the immortality of the soul, and of course in the resurrection, for one is the consequence of the other? Both of these myste-ries are based upon the intimate union between Christ and man. "Jesus," says Tertullian, "has raised our humanity to the highest

---

* De Resurrect. Carnis, c. 1.

heavens.   In the person of Jesus Christ our flesh and blood are enthroned at the right hand of the Eternal Father.   We can not deny this truth, without denying Christ's presence in heaven."   The great philosopher concludes by saying, " The Mediator who restored man to God, and brought God to man, will bring the body to the soul and the soul to the body.   Even in His own person he has joined them inseparably together for all eternity.   The body belongs to the soul, and the soul will not be deprived of its companion, its friend and brother—the body.

And thus, my dear friend, divine wisdom attains its object.   In the mystery of the resurrection, it destroys that pernicious dualism of body and soul which, by separating one from the other, deprives man of his immortality, God of His Glory, and the Incarnate Word of the fruits of redemption.

God's justice demands that we should rise from the dead.   Cemeteries are consecrated on account of the body, the body is created for the soul, the soul is created for God. Hence our reverence for the cemetery.   A body which has been closely united to a soul, the breath of God, is too sacred, in our estimation, not to be provided with a becoming resting-place after death. In fact, the doctrine of the immortality of the soul, professed as it is and believed by all nations, supposes the resurrection of the flesh.

The doctrine of future rewards and punishments necessarily depends upon the doctrine of immortality. The soul is not the whole of man. For man is a soul and body united in one person, who has done right or wrong as one person. This person, then, must be rewarded or punished ; and it is only in the reunion of soul and body by virtue of the resurrection, that man can be complete, and receive his rewards and punishments as man. This is the doctrine held by the fathers. Hear Tertullian : " Man being a free being, is responsible for his acts to the God who has given him life, and endowed him with free-will. He is bound, therefore, to render an account of the use made of these blessings; that is, he must be judged, rewarded, or punished by God Himself. This is simple justice.

" God is Judge because He is Master ; He is Master because He is Creator; and He is Creator because He is God. Man, to be justly judged, must rise again and appear before God's tribunal in his twofold capacity of soul

and body; for he is to be judged in his en-
tirety, as he had lived. He ought to be
judged as he lived, because it is about his
manner of living that there is question.
Judgment and sentence must affect all the
elements whereby he was enabled to live."
He must be judged in soul and body united.

Tertullian, insisting on the necessity of a
judgment, thus addressed the opponents of
the resurrection :

" If you pretend to divide soul from
body in the matter of reward and punishment, you must, without delay, begin at once
to take them apart in the duties and functions
of life. If there is to be no sharing of the
reward, there must be no coöperation in life.
Even when thinking, the soul acts by, with,
and through the flesh. As long as it is in
the body, it will act with it. It manifests its
very thoughts by aid of the flesh ; the countenance is its mirror. You charge the body
with wrong-doing, therefore it ought to be
punished. We count its virtues, and deem it
worthy of reward if innocent.

" Although the soul gives the impulse, and
commands the action, it is the body that exe-
cutes it. Can we believe God to be an unjust
judge, or a powerless one ? He would be un-

just if He deprived of its reward that portion of man which has had so large a share in his good works—powerless if he failed to punish its companion in iniquity."

Tertullian most unmercifully pursues into their last stronghold the "solidaires" of his time, tears their objections into tatters, and exposes to the world the secret cause, ever old and ever new, of their unbelief. Let me quote a few more of his expressions. It does one good to see him chastise with vigorous arm the pupils of doubt and incredulity.

" You assert that the flesh is a blind instrument, having no will of its own. You are mistaken. The body can not be called an instrument; for an instrument is an external implement—something foreign to the substance of man. The flesh, on the contrary, is united intimately with the soul, even in the maternal womb, clothes it, is born with it, and is associated in all its operations. St. Paul terms it the exterior man. Thus the body, being the soul's minister or co-agent, is subject to judgment. Not that it has of itself any consciousness, but because it has been made part of that which has consciousness of right and wrong—the soul.

" Now St. Paul, although he knew that what

is done by the body is attributable to the soul, yet he pronounces the body sinful; for fear that people who knew it to act under the soul's impulse, would consider it irresponsible and exempt from judgment. And again, when he attributes good works to the body, telling us, for example, to glorify and carry God in our bodies, he knows that these good works are imputable to the soul. And yet it is to the flesh he promises the reward. If this were not the case, he would have neither reproach nor encouragement to offer to the body, which would be ignorant of the differ-ence between good and evil, and consequently would have nothing to fear nor to hope for on the last day."

Tertullian concludes by revealing the secret of all this incredulity. I will conclude, too, this letter, with the words written by his powerful hand: " These calumniators of the flesh are they who love it most. No one lives so fleshly as those who deny the resurrection of the flesh. They deny this mystery because they fear it; they fear it because they desire to live according to the dictates of their vile passions."

TWENTY-SIXTH LETTER.

MY DEAR FRIEND:

God's goodness requires that we should rise again. God hates nothing that He has made. *Nihil odisti horum quæ fecisti.* On the contrary, He loves the works of His hands. See with what fatherly solicitude He protects and defends them. To the most insignificant insect, and to the smallest blade of grass, He supplies every thing requisite for its existence, its beauty, its reproduction—for the varied functions assigned to it in the plan of creation. He loves the human body, because it is His work. He loves it with special tenderness, because it is the masterpiece of His hands. All men of learning, pagan as well as Christian, who deserve to be called learned, have

been overwhelmed with admiration and de-
light in contemplating it. The beauty of
form, the dignity of attitude, the grace of motion, the intelligent and animated expression
of face, the delicate perfection of the organs ;
all serving to distinguish it from the mere
animal ; all these wonderful excellencies have
filled the physiologist's soul with ecstasy.
Galen, after he had dissected the human
finger, exclaimed, that he had just been
chanting a beautiful hymn in praise of the
Creator.

But these are the least of our body's pre-
rogatives. God was not satisfied with be-
stowing upon it external grace and beauty.
He lit it up, consecrated it, made it, so to
speak, divine, by breathing into it His own
breath. Yet men would consign to the fate
of a dead brute this palace of the soul, this
inseparable and necessary minister of its
noble operations, and with whom it shares the
sovereignty of creation.

" This body of the Christian, which has
been so often sanctified, and so often the
means of sanctifying the soul ; which, in
martyrdom, is ever the visible witness and defender of truth ; this flesh so sacred, so holy,
the brother of Christ—you would abandon for-

ever to the corruption of the grave! Where are your Christian feelings?"

"No! a thousand times no!" exclaims Tertullian, "it must not be thus. This flesh which God has made to His own image; which He animated with His own breath; which He enthroned as king of nature, sanctified by His sacraments; whose purity He loved, whose austerities He accepted, and whose sufferings He crowned; this flesh, O my God! which has been so often Thy flesh, will remain in corruption forever? No! a thousand times no!"

Moreover, God loves our body, because it is the image of His Son, the Word Incarnate, who is the eternal object of His complaisance. Now, no visible creature, except the human body, bears resemblance to the Word made flesh. When God looks down from heaven upon a sinless body, He delights in telling the astonished angels, "This is my well-beloved Son, in whom I am well pleased."

God loves the body, even in its weakness. "We know," says Tertullian, "that God is good; from Christ's words we know that He is goodness itself. For through Christ He has commanded us, first to love Himself, and then to love our neighbor; He Himself giving us the example by loving this flesh of ours, which is closely related to Him.

" You say our flesh is infirm. I grant it. But it is in infirmity that virtue attains perfection. It is diseased; physicians are required only for those who are sick. It is lost; I came, says Christ, to save that which was lost. It is a sinner; He replies, ' I will not the death of a sinner, but that he be converted and live.'

" Why afflict the flesh with those infirmities which appeal to God, which hope in Him, and which He regards by coming to their aid? I will tell you. If our flesh were free from misery, the goodness, grace, mercy, and generosity of God would be without an object."

God loves our flesh because of its sufferings. Job said that compassion was born of God. God's heart is a never-failing fountain of compassion. How often does He tell us so in the Scriptures! It is the part of a large and magnanimous heart, to show marked tenderness to a weak, suffering creature. On this ground, how strong are the claims of our body! Come, my dear Frederic, to the cradle of this newly-born infant. Look closely at this little stranger, who seems to have fallen unexpectedly on the surface of this cold and cheerless world. This little thing is yourself just twenty years ago, or perhaps it is myself some sixty years ago. It is the reader of these lines. It is every man or woman that has come into the world. It has eyes, but it does not see; ears, but it hears nothing; a mouth that can not speak; a hand which it don't know how to use; feet, but it can not walk, nor even stand erect. It knows but one thing; and that it has not learned —namely, to weep.* Other creatures are clothed at their birth; some have feathers or at least down, some have scales, some have thick fur; but all are protected by their peculiar covering, against heat and cold. Man only is born naked, and liable to every kind of suffering. Hence it is, that of all animals, he is the only one that is born weeping. Human life begins in the cradle, exists on a cross, and ends in the grave. This cross the body carries throughout the whole of its journey. It is a very heavy cross, and, unless assisted by a supernatural arm, we would sink exhausted under its weight. For it is not smoothly rounded, but rough and angular, covered with knots and sharp points. It fastens itself to man. Do what he may, he

* Plin. Hist. lib. vii. Procm.

can not shake it off. Every son of Adam
treads the weary road from his cradle to his
grave, beneath the weight of this onerous
burden. With heavy heart, tearful eyes, and
aching limbs, he drags behind a long clank-
ing chain of blighted hopes.

We have not even the comfort of owning
the whole of this life, short as it is. We enjoy it only a moment at a time. Every day,
every hour, every minute we lose a portion
of it. As we increase, it decreases. We
have lost infancy, childhood, youth. Up to
to day, to this very hour, our time is dead.
Death's icy fingers are even now clutching
the present moment—it is dying, dead, gone
forever. Whilst I say it is dead, I myself am
dying.

Who would condemn this body of ours to
such an existence? Is it thus, that God
would show His tender love for our flesh; the
masterpiece of His hand, the brother of the
Word Incarnate? Would He thus, of His
own free-will—that omnipotent, all-wise, and
all-loving Creator—treat His poor, helpless
creature?

During the last six thousand years, myriads
of human beings have come upon this earth.
They passed a few short years of what could

hardly be called life, in darkness rather than light, in struggle, in labor, in disease. Have they gone back to the nothingness from which they came? Why were they created, why did they tarry here? To seem to be born, to suffer and die, just for the sake of seeming to be born, to suffer and to die? How very worthy of Infinite Goodness!

This is not all. In order to aggravate to the utmost the tortures of our flesh, God implanted in the human heart such an unconquerable love of life, that nothing can extinguish or even weaken it. There is nothing to prevent God from supplying us with the means of satisfying this necessity. If there is to be no future resurrection of the body, then He does fail to supply the means; heartlessly, cruelly! He would have us call Him, Our Father! And this infinitely happy Father in heaven would keep His happiness to Himself, and find an absurdly savage pleasure in seeing Himself unfortunate in His creatures! The thought is impious. To affirm it, would be a blasphemy not only against God, but against reason.

We bear within ourselves, and all nature with us, invincible proofs of a coming resurrection. Nature says that we must rise again.

Read St. Paul to the Romans : " For the ex-
pectation of the creature, waiteth for the revelation of the sons of God.   For the creature
was made subject to vanity, not willingly, but
by reason of Him that made it subject, in
hope :* because the creature† also itself shall
be delivered from the servitude of corruption,
into the liberty of the glory‡ of the children
of God.   For we know that every creature
groaneth, and travaileth in pain even until
now.   And not only it, but ourselves also,
who have the first-fruits of the Spirit."§

What mean these groanings, sufferings,
and tears of nature?   They mean, that
creation has not reached its destiny in regard to material creatures, no more than it
has for men.   They mean that creation
sighs not for its destruction, but for its
renovation; crying out like man, and with
man, " Thy kingdom come."   St. Thomas
says, that all creatures have an invincible
aversion to be destroyed.   Creatures, then, in
desiring the end of the world, do not seek
their annihilation, but their renovation and

---

* With the promise of a deliverance
† Or creation.
‡ For a glorious and blessed freedom.
§ Pledge of a glorious resurrection. (Rom. 8 : 19–22.)

resurrection to true life. This is a profession of faith in the resurrection which nature never ceases to chant.

St. Augustine teaches, that our body's profession of faith in the resurrection is equally loud and continued. " My flesh," says the great doctor, borrowing the prophet's words, " cries out, I hunger and thirst for Thee, O Lord! And how does it show its hunger and thirst? By seeking to be delivered from life's burden, and its ever-recurring needs. See to what our flesh is condemned. If we do not eat, we become weak and hungry; if we do not drink, we become languid and thirsty. If we prolong our waking hours, we grow weary and succumb to sleep; if we sleep too long, we wake up unrefreshed. To eat and drink wearies us; if we stand up for a time, we grow fatigued and must sit down; if we sit too long,. we become tired and must walk. There is nothing durable in life. Everywhere fatigue, disgust, and corruption. What connection is there between these deficiencies and the resurrection promised by Our Lord? They are so many voices crying out, We hunger after incorruption. Yes, our flesh is hungry for God. A prisoner in the wilderness of this world, its every pain, its every fatigue,

means, I hunger and thirst for my resurrection." *

I.should now explain the glory and blessings of the soul and body in the resurrection.
But in our correspondence, entitled *Life is
not Life*, I have expressed all that I knew on
the subject. You have not forgotten it, and
it seems superfluous to repeat. Suffice it to
recall to your memory St. Augustine's expression, " If the prison is so beautiful, what must
be the palace ? If exile is so pleasant, what
must be our fatherland ?" " *Si tanta fecis
nobis in carcere, quid ages in palatio?*" †

Before we part, my dear Frederic, let me
review briefly our pleasant correspondence.

Up to the present time, the revolutionists
have attacked, profaned, defiled, and destroyed
churches, chapels, convents, and religious
houses. They have torn down the cross, and
divested education of every religious feature.
One little spot of earth had escaped their vandalism—*the cemetery.* They saw that their
victory was incomplete, unless they ruined
this sacred place, which embodies the fundamental mysteries of Christianity. With dia-
bolical malice, they seek to sink society, in
the nineteenth century, below the level of the

* Enarr. in Ps. Edit. Gaume. † Soliloq. c. 21. n. 1.

savage ; for even the savage respects the sanctity of a grave, believing as he does in the future existence of the soul. Under the name of " solidaires," they would exterminate every dogma of Christianity, and thus lead men to the denial of every duty flowing from such doctrines.

Society's salvation depends upon belief in a future life. This dogma, together with its deductions of immortality, resurrection, rewards and punishments, is loudly and impressively taught by the Christian cemetery ; taught in countless ways; by the sanctity of the place itself, by emblems and inscriptions, and even by its very title of cemetery, which means the resting-place of those who have fallen asleep in the Lord. The destruction of the Christian cemetery means the destruction of Christian society. To secularize it, and thus destroy its Christian meaning, is the aim of modern atheists.

Catholics ought to learn a lesson from their furious hatred. For it teaches plainly, that it has become necessary to defend this last refuge of faith against Freemasons, materialists, " solidaires," and highly developed monkeys, who seek to make themselves and us soulless clods of dirt. Of late, anti-religious funerals, conducted by the "solidaires," have become very common in France, Belgium, and many other countries of Europe. These pompous parades, in broad daylight, of materialism, are becoming as epidemic as suicide. The more vulgar and senseless they are, the more dangerous they become, by flattering the vicious instincts of corrupt men, who would be glad to have nothing to fear beyond the grave, in order to enjoy the privilege of doing what they choose on this side. To do what they choose, means to upset and destroy social institutions, with no other fear but that of the police. Every one understands that this would be the delivering up of honest citizens, together with their property, honor, liberty, and life, to the thief and assassin.

The object of the foregoing letters is to rouse all Catholics—bishops, priests, and people—to an immediate, bold, and united protest against the abolition of Christian burial; to establish the right of the Church to the ownership and guardianship of the cemetery; to show the advantages of burial in consecrated ground; to vindicate human nature, religion, and society from the aspersions of the "solidaires;" to make men hear the eloquent warnings given us by the Christian cemetery, on the dignity of our bodies, the universal brotherhood of men, the immortality of the soul, and the resurrection of the body.

God grant that my labor be not in vain!

Farewell, dear friend: pray for me!

www.ingramcontent.com/pod-product-compliance
Lightning Source LLC
Chambersburg PA
CBHW060241290526
45789CB00001B/148